The Battelle Memorial Institute Foundation 1975-1982

A History and Evaluation

THE BATTELLE MEMORIAL INSTITUTE FOUNDATION 1975–1982

A History and Evaluation

by

Thomas H. Langevin

with

Robert H. Bremner, Henry L. Hunker,
Lucia B. Findley, Carole J. Rogers,
and others

Published by the Ohio Historical Society
Columbus, Ohio
1983

Ohio Historical Society, Columbus 43211

©1983 by the Ohio Historical Society
All rights reserved. Published 1983
Printed in the United States of America

ISBN 0-87758-017-0

Gordon Battelle

This book is dedicated, as was the foundation, to the memory of Gordon Battelle and to the many men and women of Battelle whose work over the years produced the funds that made the Battelle Memorial Institute Foundation possible.

Contents

List of Figures

List of Tables

Foreword

This study of the Battelle Memorial Institute Foundation (BMIF) affords the reader a rare glimpse of a dynamic entity which, through its board and professional staff, triggered many far-reaching initiatives and programs still readily visible even though BMIF, the catalyst, is no longer on the scene. The timeliness of the issues and the freshness of the experiences inherent in a current study make this an altogether useful document for many audiences. BMIF itself commissioned this reflective analysis as a sort of institutional "report card"; the boards and executives of metropolitan foundations elsewhere will find it a helpful and stimulating point of reference as they assess their own local and regional needs and opportunities. The focus of this volume is upon metropolitan Columbus, Ohio. Regional case studies invite comparisons with other geographical districts and/or with the same area at another period of time. Similarly, the nature of BMIF, as revealed in the following pages, becomes a template alongside which other local/regional foundations might array themselves, not for the purpose of invidious contrasts but so as to test the likely relevance of environmental conditions here and any "lessons" thought to have been learned.

The interests of the Ohio Historical Society in publishing this case study deserve some exposition. A multifaceted, cultural/educational institution with a comprehensive mission embracing the history of Ohio and Ohioans, the Society has had a particular interest in contributing to the understanding of the precursors of our contemporary world. In pursuit of that objective, the Society has published, for nearly a century, a wide variety of materials embracing natural history, archaeology, and history—the common denominator being an expected contribution to general understanding of both the representative and the idiosyncratic elements of things Ohio.

Thomas H. Langevin, the principal author, and his colleagues have confronted the nettlesome tasks of differentiating opinion from verifiable fact and insuring that the importance of each is accurately captured and conveyed. Moreover, the authors address multiple audiences, including persons locally who will be especially familiar with the personalities and projects described herein; thus, the volume will be read critically and comprehended from a variety of informed perspectives.

The Society has acted upon the inspiration of the BMIF Board of Trustees who concurred in the wisdom of insuring that some complete and reasonably objective record of their decisions and stewardship was available soon after those decisions were rendered. The quest for objectivity was materially advanced by the team approach and through the methods utilized by the researchers. The significance of the work, like BMIF itself, will be discussed now and in the future. To that end, the essential next step is to read and evaluate the book so that learning may continue—to the ultimate benefit of Ohioans and others elsewhere who strive for both appreciation and betterment of what we have.

Therefore, this book conveys the thoughtful labors of able and energetic scholars who, by virtue of their diverse training and backgrounds, have melded their efforts into a more comprehensive study than any would have produced singly. Further, the bridging of disciplinary perspectives and emphases makes the narrative more broadly available to and, it is hoped, appreciated by a variety of readers.

Revealing the past, especially as that revelation allows us to under-
stand better the present, has long been the hallmark of history and of this
Society.

Gary C. Ness, Director
The Ohio Historical Society
Columbus, Ohio
December 1983

Preface

While the Battelle Memorial Institute Foundation's (BMIF) seven-year life occupied only a very short span of time in the history of central Ohio, its impact was significant.

As M. J. Rossant, director of the Twentieth Century Fund, once told me in a letter, for every observer of a foundation, there will be as many different ideas as to its meaning to the community. Other foundation executives made the same point—that the measurement of a foundation's activity can be reasonably well-determined, but the consequence of that activity is more difficult, if not impossible, to discover.

Even quantitative analysis of the results of foundation grants, although carefully secured, cannot give full evidence of their impact. In some cases, too little time has elapsed for evaluation, and some agencies keep incomplete records. Generally, agencies are not anxious to share failures or difficulties.

In the case of BMIF, however, there were conditions that made it possible to secure reasonable evidence of its impact. First, its total assets of over $22 million were distributed within a short period of time. In addition, these funds were distributed within a very limited geographic area—central Ohio. Further, as the following history shows, the BMIF board tended to make sizable grants to well-established organizations.

A continuing evaluation of BMIF's grants was not required, since the foundation funded only 501(c)(3)—not for profit—organizations and could rely on the agencies to do their own reporting as a matter of fiscal accountability under the tax laws. Also, because of the foundation's short life span, a continuing system of grant evaluation, other than the maintenance of accurate grant records, was not necessary.

Yet, the BMIF trustees wanted to see an analysis of their efforts, as well as leave behind the story of what had been accomplished. Rather than merely compiling accumulated reports of grants made, the board determined there should be an analysis and evaluation of the grants and other BMIF activities during the period of its existence. This would serve as a final report and permanent historical record of the administration of the foundation. In addition, the board directed that the history of BMIF be used to provide insight and guidance for the charitable activities of others in the future.

The preparation of the history has been the cooperative effort of associates drawn from the disciplines of history, geography, education, political science, and public administration. The research, analysis, and evaluation have used the methods of both the humanities and the social sciences.

Those who participated as my associates were Robert Bremner, my senior colleague throughout and emeritus professor of history at The Ohio State University; Henry Hunker, professor of geography and public administration at The Ohio State University and well known for his knowledge of urban affairs; Lucia Findley, who has specialized in the impact of the arts on communities; Carole Rogers, a historian with work and research experience in social agencies; Lawrence Peterson, political scientist; R. Gregory Browning, historian; Eric Lewandowski, who served as graduate assistant in history and later as research assistant; Timothy Langevin, researcher and writer; Richard Hopkins, associate professor of history at The Ohio State University, who helped in the early days of the project; Anne Peterson, who contributed research from social agencies; and Brad Quicksall, freelance writer. These scholars contributed specific pieces of work, but the work is more than a collection and editing of these separate tasks. The purpose here has been to secure the independence and integrity of individual scholarship, while at the same time blending them into a compatible whole. Hence, the names of authors do not appear in specific chapters. The cooperative nature of the venture took us beyond that.

Others also contributed to the work. A number of foundation executives and community leaders were kind enough to react to my early design of the project. Dennis Benson, president of Appropriate Solutions, Inc., aided in the construction and use of statistics; Gaylor Whitney of Whitney-Bolton & Associates also provided assistance with the statistics; and Kae Lea Main of that company did the word processing. The draft manuscript was edited by Barbara Longstreth; the final version by Ellen Kindle and Susan Leonhart.

To the work itself! There are four major parts to the history. First, there is a perspective on Columbus, Ohio, home of BMIF. Columbus can mean many things to many people, so it was essential to describe "the territory" as it was in 1975. Second, the work outlines the story of the foundation: its board, its staff, its policies, its procedures, its decisions, and its operations. Third, it covers the impact of BMIF grants on the recipients and consequently on central Ohio. Fourth, the appendix contains the survey of organizations that received grants and the statistical analysis of the grants with codes to allow interested students to probe further. A companion piece includes various documents related to the organization, operation, and dissolution of a foundation. It is hoped this rather full array of appendix material will prove useful to foundation executives and particularly to corporate executives who might be contemplating the creation of a corporate foundation.

During the conceptualization of the BMIF history project, and throughout the more than two years of research and writing done by my colleagues and me, the two major desires of the BMIF board were kept in the forefront: that the story of the Battelle Foundation be told fully and accurately, and that it be done in a way that makes its experience most useful to others.

I assume the responsibility for the work, with sincere appreciation to my associates; to the BMIF board for its confidence in supporting an independent study; and to James I. Luck, now of The Columbus Foundation, for his candid and accurate review and his support.

Special tribute is paid to the memory of Battelle's John M. Batch, BMIF trustee, a leader whose optimism and courage endured to the end in his battle against cancer, which ended in 1983.

The work is dedicated, as was the foundation, to the memory of Gordon Battelle and to the many men and women of Battelle whose work over the years produced the funds that made the Battelle Memorial Institute Foundation possible.

Thomas H. Langevin
Columbus, Ohio 1983

"

Columbus was thus fertile soil in 1975 for an investment of $22 million

"

CHAPTER I

Columbus in 1975: A Perspective

When the Battelle Memorial Institute Foundation (BMIF) was established in 1975, Columbus was in the midst of rapid change. A city that had evolved as a provincial state capital with a small-town, conservative image was experiencing dynamic growth and transformation, especially in comparison with other cities in the Northeast. Columbus was quickly maturing into a metropolis with "major city" status. This dual role of being provincial yet cosmopolitan—the latter quickly replacing the former—greeted the inception of BMIF.

The transformation of Columbus, evident to even the casual observer by 1975, was the result of many factors. But three main elements of strength—the geographic, demographic, and economic characteristics of the city—provided an undergirding for the area's growth. These elements determined the nature of changes in the cultural, social, educational, and civic sectors of the city.

1

Geographic Characteristics

Historically, Columbus stood alone on the flat central Ohio plain, relatively unencumbered by competitive urban areas. But its location on the Scioto and Olentangy rivers and its somewhat mild winters made it a logical site for a settlement long before 1812, when it became Ohio's capital. Twenty-two years later, it incorporated as a city amid its first real period of rapid development.

Columbus progressed into the twentieth century in much the same way as other northeastern cities did, with two notable exceptions. First, the city's growth took on the shape of a distorted cross, with the two arms of the cross represented by High Street to the north and Broad Street to the east. This growth was due, in part, to the prevailing transportation system, and made it difficult and expensive to provide service to separate parts of the city.

In addition, Columbus did not develop the same densely settled urban neighborhoods that characterized other industrialized cities in the state and region until the early 1900s. Missing was the tenement house (built, as a rule, to house industrial labor near a place of employment) and the traditional row house. As a result, Columbus was known very early as a city of private homes, a phenomenon that continued through 1975.

A turning point for the central business district came in 1927 with the completion of the LeVeque Tower, the city's first high-rise building. Reaching 46 stories above the street, the tower's dominance of the skyline was not to be seriously challenged for nearly 50 years. During that time, it served as an unofficial symbol of the city.

On a less lofty, but equally important level, manufacturing plants were being constructed in and around the downtown area. State government buildings, such as the State Office Building on the east bank of the Scioto, also dotted the downtown area. The city was to remain relatively small, however, until a fortuitous event occurred that would play a pivotal role in the future of the city.

It was not so much an event as it was a policy of city government. Under the leadership of Mayor Maynard E. "Jack" Sensenbrenner, the city adopted an aggressive policy that denied city water and sewer services to developing areas of the county unless they agreed to annexation by Columbus. It was a hardheaded, vigorous policy, but the results were highly positive for the city. Rather than encirclement by suburbs that sapped the city's vigor, Columbus benefited from the high concentration of population and a more solid tax base from would-be suburbs. In other cities, where industries and businesses were beyond the city's taxing boundaries, hardships resulted when the city had to bear the costs of social and human welfare problems.

In addition, the policy served to "square off" the imbalanced geographic growth of the city and reduced the problem of disjointed service areas. The city grew from 39.9 square miles just after World War II to 91.2 square miles in 1950. From 1960 to 1975, the pace slowed, but Columbus continued its policy of annexation and increased in size to 173 square miles, making it the largest city in Ohio in land area.

This growth period also brought the further development of the Columbus skyline. Expansion included construction of the Columbus Plaza Hotel (now the Sheraton Columbus), City National Bank Building (now Bank One), and RFI Insurance Building, all in the 20-story range, and all located in the center of town.

Commercial expansion also took place along Broad Street in downtown Columbus with the construction of Borden's international headquarters, the high-rise structures that housed Midland Mutual Life Insurance and Motorists Mutual Insurance Company, and the recently completed BancOhio National Bank office building near Trinity Episcopal Church on Capitol Square. The new State Office Tower, constructed during the same period, soon replaced the LeVeque Tower as the focal point of the Columbus skyline.

B y 1975, when BMIF was founded, High Street and the north side of the downtown area were on the verge of rapid expansion. By then, the Battelle Memorial Institute (BMI) commitment of $35 million to build a convention center was in place, and Nationwide Insurance Company had made the decision to build Nationwide Plaza, a striking structure that would serve as its national headquarters. A second Nationwide office building across High Street, the Ohio Center convention facility, and the Hyatt Regency Hotel would, by 1981, anchor the expansion of the north end of downtown Columbus.

During the mid-1970s, exciting developments were also taking place in the south end of the downtown area. Mayor Tom Moody had led the city government's commitment to "Capitol South," a renovation project for the deteriorating, three-square-block area immediately south of the statehouse. While a majority of the redevelopment plans were still on the drawing board in 1982, the commitment remained firm, bolstered by the completion of the "Centrum," an open-air skating rink and restaurant facility within the project boundaries. A few blocks south on High Street, another complex of government offices was completed, graced

Columbus skyline, 1983

with parks as a focal point of the development. In addition, just across Interstate 70 to the south was German Village, a historical area comprised of privately restored homes of the early German immigrants who represented a third of the population of Columbus in the mid-nineteenth century. This redevelopment of the 1960s and 1970s would serve as a model for neighborhood redevelopment efforts across the nation.

During this period, the community was also concerned about the recreational and cultural facilities available in this growing metropolitan area. The downtown area was, again, the focus of early attention. With the assistance of federal funding, the first of the "riverfront" redevelopment efforts was completed by 1973. This construction included an amphitheater and floating bandshell on the west bank of the Scioto River. In 1975, Bicentennial Park, located on the opposite side of the river, was completed with the help of private and public funding.

Another hallmark of redevelopment in the downtown area was the reclamation and restoration of the Ohio Theatre—an elegant downtown theatre building constructed in 1927. It was, however, a landmark nearly lost to the wrecking ball. In 1968, when the Loews Corporation sold the theatre to a local development company, the theatre's future appeared to be doomed. But a determined group of dedicated citizens banded together to save it, leading to the formation of the Columbus Association for the Performing Arts (CAPA). After what have been termed "incredible efforts" at fund-raising, CAPA made a down payment on the building, and in 1969 acquired the option to purchase it. Repair and refurbishing began shortly thereafter. By 1970, the Columbus Symphony Orchestra voted to move its concert series to the theatre and to double the number of concerts presented.

In March 1970, however, CAPA lacked adequate funds to pay the mortgage, and the future of the theatre again appeared dim. A $750,000 matching grant from Battelle Memorial Institute, along with a gift from the John W. Galbreath family, provided funds to retire the debt and challenged the public to match the funds and help ensure the future of the theatre. This public fund drive, the largest ever carried out in Columbus for the performing arts, brought $2.9 million from corporations and individuals and saved the Ohio Theatre.

The salvation of the Ohio Theatre also served to alert the community that the arts in Columbus were somewhat underdeveloped, and that a community-wide effort could be organized when a genuine need arose. This was exemplified by the resurrection of the Columbus Arts Council as a clearinghouse for cultural events in the city. It soon grew well beyond its charge by the Columbus Area Chamber of Commerce to stage an annual arts festival and to prepare annual calendars of cultural events. By 1971, the Greater Columbus Arts Council received corporate status as a nonprofit arts service organization and was chosen by the city of Columbus to help distribute the city's support funds to three major art institutions: the Columbus Gallery of Fine Arts (now the "Museum"), Columbus Symphony Orchestra, and CAPA. By 1975, this distribution process was still in a state of flux, but major hurdles had been overcome. The council was growing in prestige and was a reflection of an increasing awareness of the arts in Columbus.

The physical revitalization of the downtown area through construction in the 1960s and 1970s was also an indication of the increased vitality of several major service industries in Columbus. The city had evolved as an important center for real estate and development companies and banking and insurance firms. In addition, it was rapidly becoming headquarters for a number of national and statewide businesses. The prosperity that Columbus enjoyed undoubtedly played a major role in the willingness of the community to support artistic, cultural, and recreational endeavors. This, in turn, made Columbus more attractive to those businesses considering Columbus as a site for relocation.

Demographic Characteristics

It was not until the turn of the century that the population of Columbus exceeded 100,000. By 1925, it had more than doubled to approximately 260,000. In 1950, it had reached 375,000, just under three-fourths of the total county population of 503,412. By 1975, Columbus had 500,000 inhabitants, while the population of the five-county metropolitan region had, by most estimates, reached 1 million.

For the most part, the growth of Columbus was consistent with what was happening around the country. The dramatic increase and centralization of Columbus's urban population that took place in the first quarter of the century paralleled the industrial development common in many American cities. And, just as in most cities at the time, the depression brought a more modest growth that would eventually boom with the suburban growth that followed World War II.

The *pace* of change was what set Columbus apart from other cities. By 1900, Columbus was already a relatively compact city with no true suburbs. The so-called high rent district was well established along East Broad Street. The city's eastern extension across Alum Creek, into the area now known as Bexley, marked an early form of suburban development. When further expansion of suburbs to the east was slowed by industrial and commercial development, such as the 1918 construction of the government-owned Defense Construction Supply Center on East Broad Street, suburbs began to develop to the northwest in an area now known as Arlington. A relatively slow pace of suburban growth continued until World War II. During this period, communities such as Worthington and Reynoldsburg that are now contiguous to, or surrounded by, Columbus were considered suburbs or even exurbs of the city.

During the war years, people began to move to the suburbs. One significant event that led to this migration to the suburbs was the placement of the Curtiss-Wright aircraft plant in what was then countryside on East Fifth Avenue adjacent to Port Columbus Airport. The resulting expansion of residential and commercial activities in the area marked a period of rapid population growth on the east side of the city. The arrival of several other major industrial plants in Columbus following the war also stimulated movement to the suburbs. These included General Motors's Ternstedt plant and the Western Electric plant on East Broad Street. The Town and Country Shopping Center opened on East Broad Street in 1947. The first such center in the nation, it represented a response to suburban expansion. It would be a forerunner of similar and larger centers to come.

The development of the Interstate Highway System, particularly the completion of the Interstate-270 outerbelt, encouraged the outward movement of people, jobs, and services. Columbus was one of the first cities in the nation to complete its interstate highway system. The rapid expansion of suburban communities and commercial enterprises along I-270 was one of the amazing stories of growth in the mid-1970s.

While other industrialized urban areas of the Northeast had experienced decline by the 1960s and 1970s, Columbus proved to be an exception. Migration to the suburbs was evident in Columbus, but nevertheless, the central part of the city continued to experience modest growth during this period. In fact, Columbus was the only metropolitan area in the northeastern United States to grow during the period from 1960 to 1970. This has most often been attributed to the "health" of the metropolitan area and to the many factors that have been cited as the cause for this health.

Unlike other metropolitan regions, Columbus was also able to enlarge its taxing district through annexation. Its economy was not dependent on industries vulnerable to recession, such as steel, rubber, and chemicals, that prevailed in other urban settings. It did not suffer from inadequate or overcrowded highway and transit systems, and its financial stability was not burdened by a large, low-income population stranded in the inner city by the exodus of job opportunities to the suburbs.

While central Ohio has long had a high percentage of native-born citizens in its population mix, the city and the region have never had a diverse ethnic mix. As the late Ohio State University professor Wilford L'Esperance once noted, "The pot really never had a chance to melt in Columbus; it had already melted elsewhere."[1] There has been, however, a strong influence by Appalachian whites since the region's early settlement. This Appalachian migration continued through 1975, giving rise to a kind of southern ethos in the area. This settlement pattern produced a conservative trend that manifested itself in a self-reliant, independent attitude of the people toward activities such as governmental, cultural, and educational institutions. This, in turn, resulted in limited support for many of them.

At the same time, the educational institutions in Columbus were exerting a strong influence in the community. The public school system has been nationally recognized for its stability, and Columbus area colleges have long flourished. The Ohio State University has one of the largest student bodies in the nation. In addition to providing an expansive undergraduate program, it is home for well-recognized postgraduate schools. The community also has an abundance of private colleges, technical schools, and specialty institutions. The community's stable economy and high standard of living serve as tempting inducements for a number of graduates to remain in the community.

The black community of the Columbus area, which accounted for 18.5 percent of the city's population in 1970, has also contributed to the area's population mix. Unlike other cities more committed to an industrial economy, the Columbus area had not had a heavy influx of blacks during the post-World War II years. The city, however, did have a well-established stable and conservative black community that had been present for generations. Columbus lacked the labor-intensive manufacturing industries (such as steel, automobiles, and chemicals) that at one time provided entry-level jobs for black and European immigrants.

In the late 1960s and early 1970s, it became obvious that many human needs in the community were not being met. By the early 1970s, civic and government leaders were becoming conscious of the need to coordinate social service programs to uncover what resources were available, and to decide what allocation process would best distribute them. One of the key concerns was the possibility of costly duplication of service or administration.

As a result, the Metropolitan Human Services Commission (MHSC) was founded in the mid-1970s to provide information, coordination, and planning services for the entire social services system in the community. Although funding problems still exist for these organizations, particu-

8

Aerial view of The Ohio State University

larly when tax increases for funding depend upon voter approval, the founding of MHSC illustrates the broad-based concern in Columbus for social services.

Economic Characteristics

Columbus has not suffered from the social woes of other industrialized cities of the Northeast partly because of what *The Wall Street Journal* called its "20% economy—a mix of government, trade, service, and manufacturing sectors that each contribute 20% of the area's non-farm wages and salaries. The remaining 20% is a miscellany of finance, real estate, insurance, transportation, utilities, and construction."[2] Indeed, by 1960, only about 29 percent of the Columbus labor force was employed in manufacturing, a figure that would drop to 20 percent just 15 years later.

Unlike other major cities in Ohio that have grown because of industrial expansion, Columbus has built its strength upon this broadly based service economy. These activities have sparked recent economic growth and have helped minimize the problems that have typified the older industrial cities of the Northeast.

Any attempt to classify the city by type of employment leads to the conclusion that Columbus is a city with a diversified economic base. If it is dominated by a single function, one might argue that the operation of federal, state, and local governments predominates.

What is clear is that manufacturing, with its attendant problems, has not presented significant concern for the community's well-being. If anything, Columbus has suffered from a lack of the kind of large family manufacturing concerns that are known to endow a city with immense fortunes.

The decline of manufacturing in Columbus has been accompanied by expansion in the service sector of the economy. Columbus has experienced impressive growth in the areas of government, education, insurance, banking, communications, research and development, and other related services.

In addition, Columbus has developed its own set of unique home-grown industries. In many instances, local inventiveness, combined with available capital, has given rise to new industry.

At the outbreak of World War II, the city was dominated by a few large, locally owned firms, some of which were the largest in their fields. With the exception of Timken's roller bearing plant, almost no major national industry was present in the city. That changed with the arrival of the Curtiss-Wright aircraft plant in 1941, a turning point in the city's short-term and long-term future. This decision would introduce the effects of national industry and national management upon the local community in a way never experienced before.

Conclusion

At the inception of BMIF in 1975, Columbus was a community much different from the one it had been just 25 years earlier. Once a provincial state capital, dominated by a few homegrown industries and without cultural amenities, Columbus had become a community more deserving of the term "cosmopolitan." While other major urban centers around it were experiencing difficulties, Columbus was prospering during even difficult times. It emerged in the 1970s as a community willing and able to address its problems with a dynamic and positive attitude.

Columbus was thus fertile soil in 1975 for an investment of $22 million. The BMIF story that was about to unfold would prove to be a very interesting one that would have far-reaching effects on the Columbus community.

Notes

1. W. L. L'Esperance, "The Economic Ethos of Columbus, Ohio," unpublished paper, 1976. A condensed version of the paper appears in the *Bulletin of Business Research* (October 1976), Vol. LI, No. 10.

2. "Thriving Ohio Capital Seeks to Shed its Image as a Country Bumpkin," *The Wall Street Journal,* December 8, 1980.

"
*Each
board member
represented
a strong
institution and
was accustomed
to making
decisions
and exercising
authority*
"

CHAPTER II

The Foundation and Its Operations

Background and Organization

The Battelle Memorial Institute Foundation (BMIF) was the product of a lawsuit filed in 1970 by the Ohio Attorney General. The purpose of the suit was to investigate charges that trustees and officers of Battelle Memorial Institute (BMI) had failed to comply with the will of Gordon Battelle. Battelle, who died in 1923, left $1,547,000 "for the foundation of a 'Battelle Memorial Institute' . . . located in or near the city of Columbus, Ohio, for the purpose of education and research work in the making of discoveries and inventions in connection with the metallurgy of coal, iron, steel, zinc, and their allied industries."

The will also specified, but in language that proved open to various interpretations, that whenever the annual income of BMI resulted in a profit of over 20 percent on the principal of the legacy, the Board of Trustees was to distribute it to "charitable institutions, needy enterprises or persons . . . in such manner and amounts as in their judgment will do the greatest good for humanity." In addition, whenever the board became satisfied that facilities, equipment, staff, and funds were ample to ensure the purposes for which BMI had been founded and intended, all the profits over and above operating expenses were to be distributed to "worthy charitable objects and enterprises."

In the December 14, 1974, issue of *Science,* John Walsh commented, "No other research organization matches Battelle's success and at the same time operates under restrictions similar to those imposed by the will." Before 1969, the restrictions had not been so irksome nor had they impeded BMI's development as one of the largest and most important private research organizations in the United States. BMI leaders interpreted the will broadly and used earnings from research and development to build, expand, and improve the organization's plant, staff, and research capability. Forty years after BMI was founded, its original modest endowment had grown into assets worth $300 million.

In 1968, Battelle had research contracts with government and industry totaling more than $125 million. The institute maintained laboratories not only in Columbus, but also in Richland, Washington; Geneva, Switzerland; and Frankfurt, Germany. It supported a research center in Seattle, Washington, and sponsored and financed research in a wide range of areas, including social and economic concerns such as alcoholism, ghetto schools, and urban transportation. "It has about 7,000 employees and a hand in almost every scientific pie imaginable," *The Wall Street Journal* reported in a January 12, 1970, front-page article entitled "Brains for Hire." "Battelle's handiwork shows up everywhere—from an aluminum alloy in the Apollo space craft to the three-layer 'sandwich' coins in your pocket," the article said.

Critics, especially Richard B. Metcalf, judge of the Franklin County Probate Court, whose complaints led to the investigation and subsequent litigation, objected that BMI's far-flung and wide-ranging activities exceeded the scope of the endeavor outlined in Battelle's will. They also charged that BMI's management had neglected to make contributions to charities to the extent provided for in the will.

The Ohio Attorney General's office, in its study of BMI operations, adopted a stricter interpretation of the terms of the will. That interpretation would require more generous distributions to outside charities than BMI officials had been making. In January 1975, the attorney general and BMI lawyers announced an agreement that settled five years of controversy and litigation. The agreement was approved by Judge William T. Gillie of the Franklin County Court of Common Pleas on May 7, 1975, and required BMI to distribute $80 million of its assets to satisfy past obligations to charities. BMI also accepted a new formula for determining the distribution of funds to charities in the future and trust supervision by the Court of Common Pleas and the attorney general.

The $80 million settlement was an amount greater than the combined assets of all the philanthropic foundations based in Columbus and central Ohio. It was nearly 12 times larger than the goal set for the 1975 fund-raising campaign for United Way of Franklin County. The settlement included a $7.2 million credit for BMI's distribution to charities from 1956 to 1974; a $36.5 million allocation to the Battelle Commons Corporation for development of the Ohio Center; $7.7 million for a continuing BMI-sponsored program of research and development on energy sources; $7.7 million to the Academy for Contemporary Problems, an organization that was formerly sponsored by BMI and The Ohio State University, to become an independent entity; and $20.9 million to found BMIF and make one-time grants to 40 charitable, religious, educational, and civic institutions.

How decisions were reached regarding division of the $80 million among these recipients lies outside the scope of this study. It should be noted, however, that the award to the Battelle Commons Corporation for the Ohio Center, which represented more than 45 percent of the total, had been pledged by BMI before the suit was settled. This gift, combined with BMI's credit for previous distributions, the contribution to BMI's energy study, and the several grants to the Academy for Contemporary Problems, consumed almost 75 percent of the total. The $15.4 million originally earmarked for BMIF represented just less than 20 percent.

Rather than establish a new foundation, BMI considered giving the entire "outside charities" distribution to The Columbus Foundation, a public foundation that received funds from individuals, corporations, and other donors for distribution to charitable organizations. Instead, BMI donated $2 million to The Columbus Foundation to establish the Battelle Fund and gave the foundation an additional $25,000 for general operating expenses. The decision to create BMIF as a new private foundation was in accord both with the advice of Norman Sugarman, a recognized authority on charitable tax exemption whose legal services were retained by BMI to help set up the foundation, and the desire of BMI officials to memorialize Gordon Battelle by fulfilling the terms of his will through an agency of their own making.

BMIF's share of the distribution and its governance, purpose, and duration of existence were determined before the foundation was formed. In January 1975, Sherwood L. Fawcett, president of BMI, made it known that the foundation would be affiliated with five other Columbus organizations: Capital University, Children's Hospital Research Foundation, The Columbus Foundation, The Ohio State University Research Foundation, and United Way of Franklin County. These organizations, he said, represented "practically the whole spectrum of charitable activities." BMIF was intended to complement the work of these five organizations but, in Fawcett's words, not "become a part or extension of them."[1] A prospectus for the yet to be appointed trustees of the foundation, prepared by BMI lawyers and dated May 1, 1975, confirmed earlier decisions about representation on the governing board:

> The Board of Trustees of Battelle Memorial Institute Foundation shall be seven (7) in number and consist of the persons from time to time occupying the position specified in the organizations listed below:
>
> 1. The Chairman of the Board of Trustees of Children's Hospital Research Foundation of Columbus, Ohio.
> 2. The President of the United Way of Franklin County, Inc.
> 3. The President of The Ohio State University Research Foundation.
> 4. The President of Capital University.
> 5. The Assistant to the President of Battelle Memorial Institute.
> 6. The Director of the Columbus Laboratories of Battelle Memorial Institute.
> 7. The member of the governing committee of the Columbus Foundation appointed by the Judge of the Probate Court of Franklin County.
>
> Trustees shall serve so long as they remain in the positions specified.

The prospectus also outlined the donor's general and specific concerns regarding distribution of funds by BMIF:

> The primary purpose is to enhance organizations and people of the Central Ohio Community. It is considered that first recognition should be given to the utilization of these dollars for seed money that will proliferate into capital improvement programs in the Central Ohio area. The Deed of Gift in establishing the Foundation will indicate that among the purposes of the gift shall be education in all branches of learning, scientific research, and improving the quality of life. Particular consideration shall be given to:
>
> 1. Benefits to residents of the Central Ohio area.
> 2. Assisting students to obtain an education.
> 3. Challenge grants, as opposed to grants for uses which require no contributions by others.
> 4. Grants made in a manner which does not discourage other giving, but rather as a means of supplemental giving.
> 5. Grants to specific projects or activities as opposed to general grants for unspecified activities.
> 6. Distribution of substantially all of the Founding Contribution and income thereon in a period of not less than five (5) nor more than ten (10) years from the date of this agreement.

The prospectus also called on the trustees to develop criteria "to ensure the most prudent utilization of the available dollars within the Central Ohio area," and it repeated that a reasonable time period for distribution of funds was five to ten years after its establishment. The document authorized the trustees to employ a paid executive and administrative staff "with experience in foundations" to assist in developing and implementing the work of the foundation.[2]

On May 20, 1975, BMIF was incorporated as a charitable corporation under the nonprofit corporation laws of Ohio. The articles of incorporation stated, "This Corporation is organized and shall be operated exclusively for charitable, educational, and scientific purposes by making grants to organizations and individuals, exclusively in furtherance of such purposes." Another section declared, "It is intended that this Corporation shall have and continue to have the status of a corporation which is exempt from federal income taxation under Section 501(c)(3) of the Internal Revenue Code of 1954. . . . "[3]

The first trustees were appointed on May 30, 1975, and they held the positions specified both in the prospectus and articles of incorporation. They were: John W. Kessler, president, Board of Trustees, Children's Hospital Research Foundation; Clyde R. Tipton, Jr., president, United Way of Franklin County; Albert J. Kuhn, president, The Ohio State University Research Foundation; Thomas H. Langevin, president, Capital University; G. C. Heffner, assistant to the president, community affairs, BMI; John M. Batch, director, Columbus Laboratories, BMI; and James Petropoulos, member, governing committee, The Columbus Foundation. Kessler, Heffner, and Petropoulos continued on the board throughout BMIF's existence; Kuhn and Langevin served for four years, Batch for three, and Tipton for ten months.

The trustees brought a strong combination of entrepreneurial and managerial experience to the foundation and a knowledge of and involvement in community affairs. Two were successful businessmen —Kessler headed a nationally known real estate consulting, investing, and financing firm, and Petropoulos owned a company that specialized in the appraisal and sale of large commercial and industrial properties. Kuhn was provost and chief academic officer of The Ohio State University, and Langevin was president of a highly regarded, private church-related university. Tipton, although he did not represent Battelle on the board, was vice president of communications at BMI. Batch, who came to Columbus in 1973 from Battelle's Pacific Northwest Laboratories, was a mechanical engineer with a background in teaching, research, administration, and research management. Before retiring from active duty in 1975, Heffner, a career naval officer with the rank of rear admiral, had been commanding officer of the Columbus Defense Construction and Supply Center.

With the exception of Batch, all the trustees, by 1975, had been residents of Columbus for five or more years. Because of their position and prominence, all had been active in organizations such as United Way, the Boy Scout Council, Columbus Gallery of Fine Arts, Columbus Symphony Orchestra, Columbus Association for the Performing Arts, United Negro College Fund, and Goodwill Industries. At the time of their appointments to the BMIF board, the trustees ranged in age from 39 to 56. Kessler and Petropoulos had bachelor's degrees from The Ohio State University; Tipton had a master's in metallurgical engineering from the University of Kentucky; Heffner held a master of business administration degree from Stanford; and Batch (Purdue, mechanical engineering), Langevin (Nebraska, history), and Kuhn (Johns Hopkins, English) had doctorates.

At the board's first meeting on June 3, 1975, the trustees elected Heffner, who had helped plan the foundation, as president. Langevin was elected secretary, and Kessler was named treasurer. These officers served until October 31, 1976. After that time, terms of office ran from November 1 to October 31. The board chose William L. Clark of Knepper, White, Richards & Miller as legal counsel.

One of Heffner's first actions as president was to apply for exemption from federal income tax under Section 501(c)(3) of the Internal Revenue Code. Exempt status was in accordance with the intention of the foundation's articles of incorporation and was necessary for transfer of BMI's contribution to the foundation. BMIF's application, approved on July 3, 1975, authorized grants both to exempt and nonexempt organizations. However, attorney Robert S. Bromberg of Baker, Hostetler and Patterson, the Cleveland law firm that handled the application, advised BMIF to use "extreme caution" and avoid "making any grants to organizations other than those holding rulings or determination letters under Section 501(c)(3)." Bromberg's advice, contained in a letter to Heffner dated June 19, 1975, appears to have been a decisive factor in leading BMIF to adopt the policy of awarding grants only to organizations exempt under Section 501(c)(3) of the Internal Revenue Code.

BMI's deed of gift, accepted by the foundation's trustees on July 7, 1975, transferred no funds to the foundation and did not indicate how much would be donated. It did, however, define the terms under which "the founding contribution" would be used when it was made. In language stronger than that used in the prospectus, the deed stated that the use of the founding contribution should be limited to "education in all

18

19

Mrs. Robert H. Jeffrey, II

President
Board of Trustees
United Way of Franklin County, Inc.
BMIF Board: 1976-77

John W. Kessler

Chairman of the Board
Children's Hospital
Research Foundation
BMIF Board: 1975-82
Treasurer: 1975-76
President: 1976-77

Albert J. Kuhn

President
Board of Directors
The Ohio State University
Research Foundation through
September 25, 1979
BMIF Board: 1975-79
Secretary: 1977-79

Ralph C. Kunze

President
Board of Trustees
United Way of Franklin County, Inc.
BMIF Board: 1977

Thomas H. Langevin

President
Capital University through
August 31, 1979
BMIF Board: 1975-79
Secretary: 1975-77
President: 1977-78

Richard F. Luecht

President
Board of Trustees
United Way of Franklin County, Inc.
BMIF Board: 1979-80
Treasurer: 1979-80

James Petropoulos

Member
Governing Committee
The Columbus Foundation
BMIF Board: 1975-82
Treasurer: 1976-78
President: 1978-79

Robert H. Potts

President
Board of Trustees
United Way of Franklin County, Inc.
BMIF Board: 1980-82
Treasurer: 1980-82

W. Ann Reynolds

President
Board of Directors
The Ohio State University
Research Foundation
effective September 26, 1979
BMIF Board: 1979-82
Secretary: 1980-82

22

Harvey Stegemoeller

President
Capital University
effective September 1, 1979
BMIF Board: 1979-82
Secretary: 1979-80
President: 1980-81

Clyde R. Tipton, Jr.

President
Board of Trustees
United Way of Franklin County, Inc.
BMIF Board: 1975-76

Edward W. Ungar

Director
Columbus Laboratories
Battelle Memorial Institute
BMIF Board: 1978-82
Treasurer: 1978-79
President: 1979-80

branches of learning, scientific research, and improving the quality of life." It said grants should also be substantially limited "to those benefiting Central Ohio," an area defined in the deed as Franklin County and the adjacent counties of Madison, Fairfield, Licking, Delaware, Union, and Pickaway. As in the prospectus, the deed asked the trustees to give particular consideration to "assisting students to obtain an education," grants that would stimulate giving by others, and grants for specific projects rather than for general or unspecified activities. It also requested that distribution of substantially all of the founding contribution take place in a period of no less than five years and no more than ten years from the date of the agreement. The deed permitted BMIF to make grants to BMI-created organizations, such as the Academy for Contemporary Problems. However, it prohibited grants to BMI itself or to organizations controlled by BMI, its officers, trustees, employers, or members of their families.[4]

BMI's founding contribution, received by the foundation during July and August, consisted of stock, treasury bills, cash, and mortgage notes amounting to approximately $18.9 million.[5] At the July 7, 1975, meeting of the board, the trustees decided to convert the portfolio of investments into government securities and certificates of deposit issued by banks and savings institutions that met the requirements of the deed of gift. Along with the founding contribution, Battelle transferred to the foundation requests for assistance that had been accumulating since late 1974. Thus, by midsummer 1975, just months after its inception, BMIF already had a backlog of requests for $13 million from 168 individuals and organizations.

Typical of those original requests were applications from the Academy of Model Aeronautics, Washington, D.C., for a contribution to a scholarship program for outstanding young modelers, and from Arrow National Headquarters, also in Washington, for support of medical-surgical services for native Americans. The Therapeutic Handwriting Research Project of Columbus asked for "any part of $37,340" for "changing attitudes through changing handwriting techniques." The applications ranged in size from $750 for the Knox County (Ohio) Hunger Committee, to Southern Connecticut State College's application for $1 million for "investment purposes," and Scioto Society's $4 million request to develop a "Wilderness Ohio" complex in the Chillicothe area.

Other proposals received by BMIF in July and August included several for "assisting students to obtain an education." Two such requests asked assistance for a young Columbus woman who wanted to continue her college studies and for expansion of a church-operated academy in Columbus.

Both The Columbus Foundation and the Academy for Contemporary Problems offered to help BMIF develop procedures and guidelines for awarding grants. They also offered assistance with research and evaluation of grant applications.

At their second meeting, the trustees decided to employ a consultant from outside Columbus who could offer advice on distribution criteria, operating procedures, and personnel needs. On the recommendation of Robert Goheen, chief executive officer of the Council on Foundations, Heffner asked Merrimon Cuninggim, former president of the Danforth Foundation and advisor to the Ford Foundation on program management, to prepare a report for submission to the trustees at their meeting on August 26.

By the time Cuninggim arrived in Columbus, BMIF had leased office space at 100 East Broad Street in downtown Columbus and had hired its first employee, Mary Ellen Gruber, to serve as administrative assistant to the Board of Trustees. She later became its administrative officer. During visits to Columbus in July and August, Cuninggim interviewed members of the board and a number of community leaders, including Sherwood L. Fawcett of BMI; Mayor Tom Moody; James A. Norton, chancellor of the Ohio Board of Regents; John A. Ellis, superintendent of Columbus Public Schools; Jack Gibbs of the Ft. Hayes Career Center; Walter Tarpley of the United Community Council; Frank Lomax of the Urban League; Kline Roberts of the Columbus Area Chamber of Commerce; Mrs. Robert H. Jeffrey, II, and Alfred Dietzel of United Way; and William Guthrie, chairman, and Richard Oman, director, of The Columbus Foundation.[6]

Cuninggim's report cited problems facing the foundation, outlined suggested criteria for awarding grants, and defined program fields and operating policies. Among the problems the report cited were BMIF's "inadequately representative Board" that included "no women, no labor, no blacks, etc.," and BMIF's limited period in which to distribute its endowment. Cuninggim noted that the foundation's short life expectancy was a limitation that had been imposed by BMI rather than by the court. He recommended four key program areas—education, conservation, community services, and the arts—as appropriate for foundation funding. He also suggested several other areas, including housing and rehabilitation and/or minority economic development and health care delivery as worthy of serious consideration. Cuninggim advised the trustees to request that The Columbus Foundation staff screen the applications already received and evaluate them in accordance with criteria and fields determined by BMIF. He also recommended that the foundation employ an executive director who would be able to determine later if additional staff members would be needed. In addition, it was suggested that BMIF make use of the expertise of The Columbus Foundation, "the only exclusively grant-making, professionally administered philanthropy in Columbus."[7]

Cuninggim's report and the issues it raised were the subject of an all-day session of the board on October 20. This meeting was attended by Mrs. Robert H. Jeffrey, II, president-elect of United Way. A series of trial votes found the trustees neither unanimous nor strongly divided in their views. They generally agreed that BMIF should devote from 80 to 90 percent of its funds to local causes, as opposed to those that were statewide or national. The foundation, they felt, should try to complete its work in five to seven years and should adopt a ceiling of $1 million on individual grants. They also agreed there should be a minimum amount for small grants, but were unable to decide on the exact figure. Different trustees set the proposed minimum at $1,000 to $25,000. Two members suggested that no more than $1 million be awarded in 1975, others suggested $750,000 to $500,000, one said "very little," and one suggested the "IRS minimum." The trustees agreed on the desirability of hiring an executive director, on the use of the matching-grant device whenever possible, on not making grants for operating budgets, and on encouraging, but not reserving funds for grants for "new ideas." The board did not adopt Cuninggim's recommendation that the board's chief concern should be the "disestablished and disadvantaged." One trustee, however, included "improving quality of life for the disadvantaged" as a major item in the proposed areas of concentration. Individual trustee responses to the question of what *should* be BMIF's chief concern included the following suggestions:

- Franklin County Services and Building plus the small activities that help.
- Values, especially directed toward enhancement of American quality of life, particularly seeing Columbus as a national "laboratory."
- Get something unique if possible.
- To provide endowment (capital funds) in *areas* of concern, i.e., arts, community services, etc., which would generate good citizen leadership and expenditure of annual income and which will go to satisfy operating needs on the "long haul."
- Make some significant human impact, some societal gain, some measurable or discernible influence on the quality of life.
- To maximize the funds we have available to "make things happen" that would otherwise not come to pass.

In considering areas of concentration for BMIF, the trustees endorsed all the program fields Cuninggim had suggested except "housing and rehabilitation and/or minority economic development."

Decisions reached by the trustees at the meeting were incorporated into two documents: "Internal Policy Statement for Screening Applications," intended for use within the foundation, and "Published Information for Screening Applications," circulated to applicants during BMIF's first year of awarding grants. These two documents outlined the board's general intentions and identified specific points that were destined to become important parts of BMIF's grant policy. One of those was a statement that grants would be made only to organizations exempt under Sections 501(c)(3) and 509(a) of the Internal Revenue Code, and no grants would be made to individuals or for routine operating needs, budget deficits, or religious purposes.[8]

The trustees authorized Heffner to begin interviewing candidates for the position of program coordinator and adopted a resolution turning over all pending applications to The Columbus Foundation to be screened and returned to BMIF in three groups:

1. Proposals that do not meet BMIF criteria, and why.
2. Proposals that meet BMIF criteria but are not being recommended for funding by The Columbus Foundation, and why.
3. Proposals that meet BMIF criteria and are being recommended for funding by The Columbus Foundation, and why.

Heffner called the October 20 session of the board "our marathon, clean-up, decision-making meeting."[9] It brought the organizing stage of the foundation to a close and paved the way for BMIF's first venture in awarding grants.

Getting Under Way, 1975-76

The Columbus Foundation, established in 1943, was the second largest of the 11 community foundations in Ohio. At the end of 1975, it had assets of $25.5 million and was the largest philanthropic foundation in Columbus. During that year, it distributed approximately $1.5 million through 625 grants ranging up to $100,000. Because of its size and seniority, The Columbus Foundation was regarded as the city's clearinghouse for charitable activities. It offered counsel, advice, and the benefit of its experience to new organizations. During the summer of

1975, Richard Oman of The Columbus Foundation provided formal and informal assistance to Heffner in inaugurating BMIF operations. Together with Leeda Marting, assistant director of The Columbus Foundation, he also helped Ellen Gruber become oriented as administrative officer of the new foundation.

Within a week after the October 20 board meeting, The Columbus Foundation staff, including Oman, Marting, and Elizabeth Deinhardt, began reviewing the 306 inquiries and grant proposals received by BMIF. There were 125 requests from Franklin County, 59 from Ohio outside Franklin County, and 82 from states other than Ohio. Many were easily eliminated since they did not meet BMIF criteria. Some were simply inquiries or contained insufficient information, and others duplicated requests reviewed by The Columbus Foundation. BMIF paid no fee for the reviews conducted by Oman and his staff since The Columbus Foundation had agreed to use the interest earned on the Battelle Fund in 1975 to pay for services rendered to BMIF.[10] The review consisted of studying the formal applications, holding conferences with staff and board members of requesting agencies, making site visits, contacting professionals knowledgeable about the field specific to the grant request, and finally, meeting with the staff to consider the proposal and the information the primary researcher had obtained. Thus, all recommendations were essentially the result of a group decision.

The Columbus Foundation's report, submitted on November 24, 1975, a week before BMIF's first board meeting to award grants, contained a docket of 63 requests that had survived the review process. The staff advised against making any grant in 31 cases, nearly half of the total. The report recommended approval of 25 grants in specified amounts totaling $1.7 million and made no recommendations regarding six applications that involved policy issues to be resolved by the board.

Oman and his assistants recognized that the board and staff might arrive at different conclusions regarding the advisability of grants where the applications met BMIF criteria, and they made the following statement: "From your own observation of the community and its needs and your own first-hand knowledge of some of these requests, you may form conclusions which are different from those of staff. The judgment and experience which you bring to the meetings and to your analysis of this document are very important in the decision-making process."[11] These comments signified more than a conventional expression of deference. In many cases, members of the board, because of involvement in Columbus's civic, cultural, and social life, had access to information about applicants and requests not available to the staff. At the first grant meeting and throughout the foundation's life, BMIF trustees relied heavily on information, analyses, and evaluations prepared by the BMIF staff. However, they did not hesitate to follow their own conclusions when they seemed more convincing than staff recommendations. The board followed all of the staff's "no grant" recommendations at the December 1975 meeting, reduced the size of the award recommended by the staff in four cases, denied seven requests recommended for approval, postponed one, and denied the other five requests on which the staff had made no recommendation.

The 17 grants approved by the board totaled about $1.2 million. The largest share, $750,000, went to six capital fund requests for facilities construction and improvement, including $480,000 to the Columbus YMCA and $150,000 to South Side Settlement House. Of the $350,000 awarded to six community service agencies, the largest amount, $200,000, went to United Way of Franklin County to develop a comprehensive social service delivery system for Columbus. The smallest grant, $10,000, was awarded to the Central Ohio Radio Reading Service to purchase receivers for the blind and visually handicapped users of the service. Grants for education and the arts were limited both in size and number because the foundation board had not yet determined the direction it intended to follow in these areas.

Four of the 17 grants were made on a matching basis, three were contingent upon the agencies raising an equal amount from other sources, and one required the agency to raise twice as much.

The most important precedent established at the December 1975 meeting was that of denying grants for religious purposes. The issue was raised by a request from Capitol Square Ministries of Trinity Church, Inc., a nonprofit subsidiary of a downtown church. Their request for $100,000 was to fund a capital campaign to renovate the church. One purpose of the renovation was to develop the Capitol Square Program, which provided inexpensive lunches, lectures, entertainment, forums, and seminars for persons working in the downtown area. The staff report recognized that the program offered much-needed services, but suggested that the board consider whether it wished to make a commitment toward the capital needs of an institution whose principal mission was religious. In accordance with a decision made at the October 20 meeting that prohibited grants for religious purposes, the board denied the request. The policy did not preclude grants to church-related agencies as long as they did not conduct religious services on their premises. The BMIF board made or announced additional decisions regarding grant policy during the winter of 1975-76.

At its meeting on January 5, 1976, the board formally reaffirmed its policy of denying grants for operating needs "except in special circumstances" and agreed to limit grantees to a single award and to prohibit grantees to reapply until at least a year after the original grant. During the February meeting, William Clark, the board's counsel, brought up a potential problem. Since a simple majority of the trustees constituted a quorum for the transaction of foundation business, it would be possible for a grant to be awarded on the basis of as few as three affirmative votes with five members in attendance. To prevent this, the board adopted a resolution that required the affirmative vote of at least four trustees for approval of any grant.

Other problems occupied BMIF during 1976. It was necessary to select a senior staff member to conduct in-house evaluations, develop a scholarship program, and promote efforts to coordinate planning and funding of the arts in Columbus. At the January 5, 1976, meeting, the board appointed a subcommittee to define criteria and qualifications for the new staff position and authorized the sum of $5,000 to conduct the search. The duties of this program coordinator were to evaluate grant applications, prepare dockets for board meetings, conduct postgrant follow-ups, administer office operations, inaugurate proactive proposals, and advance BMIF public relations. Qualifications for the job included at least a bachelor's degree, responsible work experience in a related field, and personal qualities such as dependability, responsibility, and good judgment—"a congenial person able to get along with people yet with the capability of being firm. . . . " The subcommittee said, "The Program Coordinator must fully understand that he is accepting a position that has a life span of five to ten years. He is not being hired to establish a BMIF dynasty, but to eventually work himself out of a job."[12]

The short life expectancy of the position did not deter applicants. Even before the subcommittee's report reached the board on February 2, 30 individuals had submitted applications. An announcement of the opening was published in Columbus newspapers on February 4, and a request for assistance in publicizing it was sent to the Council on Foundations. These activities yielded further applications, bringing the total to nearly 50 by the end of March.

W. Bruce Evans, who learned about the opening from David Freeman, president of the Council on Foundations, was not among the original candidates. However, his impressive credentials and a successful interview made him the trustees' unanimous choice for what was originally called program coordinator. Evans, who was then the executive director of the Atlantic Richfield Foundation in Los Angeles, had seven years of experience in grants management, previous work experience in public relations, and a bachelor's and master's degree in business administration from Drexel University. Each trustee consented to an offer of employment made to Evans in a letter from Heffner dated April 26, 1976. Evans accepted the offer and began his duties with BMIF just before the trustees meeting on June 7, 1976.

"Assisting students to obtain an education" was one area singled out in the deed of gift as deserving of particular consideration by BMIF. Instead of simply responding to individual requests for assistance, the board decided to formulate a proactive scholarship plan. At the October 20, 1975, meeting, the trustees asked Kuhn and Langevin to prepare recommendations on current directions and needs in the field of scholarship. Langevin reported at the December 1 meeting that middle-income families had the most urgent need for college scholarships. Many programs funded from both public and private sources provided financial aid to low-income students, but middle-income students from families ineligible for scholarships based on financial need found their freedom of choice limited. Many could not afford the high tuition charged at private institutions.

While developing a proposal to submit to the board, Kuhn and Langevin used the consultation services of Joseph Kauffman, professor of higher education at the University of Wisconsin; Novice G. Fawcett, president emeritus of The Ohio State University; and John D. Millett, former chancellor of the Ohio Board of Regents. Their report, "Initiatives in Leadership for Tomorrow," discussed at the November 1, 1976, board meeting, called for a "proactive BMIF program for education" involving endowments of $1.5 million for scholarships to allow Columbus area students with leadership potential to attend Franklin County institutions. It also called for $2 million for institutional changes to meet future leadership needs. All public and private, nonprofit educational institutions in the metropolitan Columbus area would be eligible to apply for these grants.

The report recognized the national concern for leadership shown during the bicentennial year and declared that the cultivation of future leaders should be one of the special purposes of higher education. "Merit, irrespective of financial need, must be sought out. It also needs to be nourished, supported and rewarded. We propose a scholarship program for students attending four-year baccalaureate Franklin County colleges and universities based on the recognition, support and development of leadership potential."[13] The board approved the scholars program in

31

The Battelle Scholars Program is presented to area college and university presidents.

principle, extending it to include colleges and universities not only in Franklin County, but also in adjacent counties. However, it tabled the grant program for institutional change.

The Battelle Scholars Program was formally approved by the trustees on December 6, 1976, and was endowed at the level of $2 million. Its purpose was to attract and allow students with the highest leadership potential to attend colleges and universities in central Ohio. The endowment was distributed among eight institutions on the basis of "enrollment in baccalaureate and professional programs, tuition costs and previous BMIF support." In accordance with this formula, the largest portion of the endowment, $656,000, went to The Ohio State University. Capital University received $330,000; Denison University, $263,000; Otterbein College, $198,000; Ohio Wesleyan University, $198,000; Ohio Dominican College, $132,000; Columbus College of Art and Design, $65,000; and Franklin University, $33,000, which was subsequently increased to $66,000. Administrative costs for the program were estimated at $125,000. The first policy announced by the board asked participating institutions to recruit, identify, and select recipients with unusual strengths and promise in their chosen fields of study. The second directive said, "A major consideration for being selected a Battelle Scholar will be related to potentiality for leadership, and involve more than intellectual promise." The policies issued by the board provided no guidelines for identifying leadership potential, but indicated that the trustees regarded it as distinct from "intellectual promise." Experience in administering the program is discussed later in this report in "Battelle Scholars Program and Higher Education."

BMIF intended—and was expected—to make generous donations to the arts as a way of improving the quality of life in central Ohio. From the beginning, the foundation was, in Heffner's words, "besieged" by requests from music, art, drama, and dance groups. Heffner and other members of the board agreed that in order to make wise decisions on these requests, efforts should be made to coordinate the planning and funding of the many Columbus agencies involved in cultural activities. At the board's second grant meeting, held in March 1976, the trustees approved large grants to the Columbus College of Art and Design and the Columbus Association for the Performing Arts. The board postponed action on the request of the Columbus Symphony Orchestra for $2 million to be made available over a period of ten years.

In May, after Heffner had conferred with Nancy Hanks of the National Endowment for the Arts and had discussed the matter with

33

local civic and business leaders, he concluded that an outside group should review the status of the arts in Columbus. On June 7, 1976, the board approved Heffner's recommendation that the newly organized Arts Research Task Force of the Columbus Junior League be asked to conduct a study and make recommendations on how to coordinate the arts in Franklin County. The original amount of $4,000 set aside for the study proved inadequate, and on November 1, 1976, the board approved an application from the Junior League for $31,200 to support an assessment of the arts to be made by the Arts Development Association, Inc., of Minneapolis and New York. The progress and results of this study are discussed in "The Arts and Humanities."

Process of Awarding Grants

E xcept in the case of proactive grants, such as the Battelle Scholars Program, the process of awarding a grant began with the organization's application. BMIF adopted the screening procedures developed by The Columbus Foundation and set March 31, June 30, September 30, and December 31 as the closing dates for requests to be considered during the following quarter. The foundation had no specific printed application. After the initial backlog of requests had been processed, however, BMIF required each applicant to submit a written application. That application had to include, in a specified order, comprehensive information about the agency, its officers and staff, and the amount, objective, and proposed use of the grant. A mimeographed information sheet, replaced in 1977 by the brochure *Criteria for Application,* outlined 13 points of information required in all applications. These points remained unchanged throughout the life of the foundation. The first action taken by BMIF staff when an application was received was to discover whether the document contained the essential elements called for in *Criteria for Application.*

The initial screening decision, to reject outright or to proceed with a staff review, was based on three considerations: relationship of the request to the foundation's policy and program focus; size of the request in relationship to the foundation's policy and program interests; and the applicant's tax status as indicated by a letter from the Internal Revenue Service classifying the organization as tax-exempt. Requests denied by the staff without review included a brief notation such as, "outside central Ohio," "request for operating expenses," or "request identical to one already denied." Ordinarily such denials were final, although if a trustee indicated a wish to have one considered, it could be added to the docket for the next board meeting.

For applications that were complete and had survived the first screening, further review involved a ten-step process in which staff members were required to do the following:

1. Secure detailed financial information showing sources of all funds.
2. Consult with an attorney, if necessary, to determine applicant's tax status and the effect of a grant on its future tax status.
3. Evaluate the utility and promise of the project, using outside consultants if necessary.
4. Review the adequacy of the applicant's evaluation plan.
5. Judge the project timetable and cost estimates for realism and economy.
6. Analyze the funding plan: Potential for funding elsewhere? Joint funding, with other foundations? With government? What is the likelihood of future funding from other sources if the project is meant to be continuing?
7. Talk with the applicant and the principals of the project.
8. Consider the applicant's ability to execute the project, including qualifications of key personnel.
9. Make a site visit whenever possible.
10. Determine whether the project *unnecessarily* duplicates efforts of other organizations and/or individuals?[14]

After reaching a decision to recommend approval, rejection, or postponement, the staff prepared a one- or two-page summary of the proposal describing the program, budget, objective, amount requested, and the action recommended to the board.

In the early period when BMIF had no full-time professional staff, requests were submitted to the foundation's counsel, William Clark, for approval of legal issues. After W. Bruce Evans's appointment as program coordinator in July 1976, the staff submitted requests recommended for approval to Clark before the meetings to determine whether the grants constituted "qualifying distributions" by BMIF under applicable provisions of the Internal Revenue Code.

The board held grant meetings four times a year, in March, June, September, and December. Approximately two weeks before the meeting, each trustee received a docket of requests to be considered, along with a summary showing the amounts requested, purpose of grants, staff recommendations, and an analysis of each request. In the years from 1976 to 1978, when the average number of requests considered at each quarterly meeting was nearly 35, the trustees had a demanding assignment to complete before the meeting. When assembled, the board had to vote to grant, deny, or modify all requests the staff recommended for approval. It did not discuss applications for which the staff recommended no grant, unless a trustee specifically asked that it be reviewed, or because circumstances seemed to warrant board consideration.

The Columbus Foundation staff continued to review BMIF grant applications through the September 1976 grant meeting, the fourth and last of BMIF's first fiscal year. Evans participated in the review for the September meeting, and in January 1977, the board changed his title to executive director. He and Ellen Gruber were responsible for all staff reviews until the end of 1979. Gruber resigned effective September 1979 and Evans effective January 1980. James I. Luck, executive director, and Pamela Faccinto, executive secretary, constituted the foundation's staff from 1980 to 1982.

In reviewing requests, the BMIF staff conducted interviews with applicants, made site visits, exchanged information about applications, anticipated actions with The Columbus Foundation, and consulted individuals in a variety of outside agencies. These agencies included the Metropolitan Human Services Commission, Greater Columbus Arts Council, United Way of Franklin County, Mid-Ohio Regional Planning Commission, Mid-Ohio Health Planning Federation, Ohio Historical Society, Academy for Contemporary Problems, Metropolitan Park District of Columbus and Franklin County, Columbus Recreation and Parks Department, Columbus Public Schools, and Columbus and Ohio Departments of Economic Development. Sometimes a request was in an area in which a trustee had special knowledge, and Evans and Luck did not hesitate to ask trustees for suggestions or leads to be investigated.

The foundation's decision-making process involved careful and detailed staff work, prepared agendas, predistribution of staff analyses and recommendations, and comprehensive homework before board meetings. Staff recommendations were an essential, but not always decisive, factor in the process. At least one major grant decision, the establishment of the Battelle Scholars Program, was made without consulting the staff. The board frequently relied on its staff to provide information about many agencies, proposed programs, and possible duplication or overlap of services. In five and one-half years of awarding grants, the board rejected 43 requests that the staff had recommended for approval and approved 24 requests for which the staff recommended no grant. The board approved seven for more than the amount recommended by the staff. Eighteen received less than the staff recommendation.

W. Bruce Evans
Executive Director
1976-79

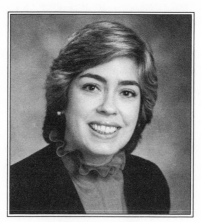

M. Ellen Gruber
Administrative Officer
1975-79

Three of BMIF's six presidents—G. C. Heffner (1975-76; 1981-82), John Kessler (1976-77), and James Petropoulos (1978-79)—served on the Board of Trustees from beginning to end. Thomas Langevin (1977-78), the foundation's third president, and Harvey Stegemoeller (1980-81) both represented Capital University. Edward W. Ungar, president from 1979 to 1980, was director of the Columbus Laboratories of BMI. Kessler, Petropoulos, Ungar, Richard Luecht, and Robert Potts served terms as treasurer. Langevin, Albert Kuhn, Stegemoeller, and Ann Reynolds served as secretary. The foundation retained a fiscal agent and accounting firm to handle financial matters. Gruber, Evans, and Luck recorded minutes of board meetings. Clark reviewed and sometimes suggested revisions in the wording of both the minutes and the grant agreements. An executive committee consisting of the president, secretary, treasurer, and executive director met occasionally, but exercised little power since the trustees preferred to keep authority within the control of the entire board.

Heffner was by far the most active of the presidents. During his initial tenure, he performed the duties of executive director as well as presiding officer at board meetings. He conferred often with The Columbus Foundation staff to ensure that questions had been answered. In sensitive or controversial cases, he recommended action short of outright rejection of proposals to permit resubmission at a later date. In October 1976, at the end of his first term as president, Heffner estimated that he had devoted over 200 hours, or 18 hours per month, to his duties. He continued to keep in close touch with BMIF's executive directors even after leaving office to raise questions about staff recommendations or to indicate disagreement with those recommendations.

After Evans assumed the responsibility of executive director, it was not necessary for Kessler and subsequent presidents to be as involved in the day-to-day operations of the foundation. However, each served as the link between the staff and the board, approved agendas for board meetings, and made a distinct contribution to the foundation's record. The problems and decisions of their administrations are discussed further in "Major Grant Decisions."

No president, no matter how effective or respected, dominated the Board of Trustees. Each board member represented a strong institution and was accustomed to making decisions and exercising authority. Had the board been constructed differently, members might have spent more time and energy on struggles for power and precedence. Since trustees were selected on the basis of institutional position, and faced a specific mission within a specified time frame, they could go about their task with a minimum of friction and with mutual esteem, respect, and goodwill.

The realization of high community expectations and a sense of involvement in decisions that would affect the future of a community imparted zest and excitement and inspired a feeling of fellowship. Since the seven trustees were generally in agreement about objectives and methods, differences of opinion—and even heated arguments about individual cases—did not cause animosity among members.

The board's composition represented an interesting and valuable interplay of professional expertise. Trustees recognized and relied on the special knowledge of other trustees. Kuhn, Langevin, and later Reynolds and Stegemoeller relied on Kessler and Petropoulos on questions of property and building costs; in turn, other trustees expected Kuhn, Langevin, Reynolds, and Stegemoeller to provide advice on educational matters. Kuhn later observed that, although he was willing to take advantage of the expertise of individual members, "The dynamics of the Board was such—in its candor, informality and commonality of aspiration for the Foundation—that major and minor items generally received the full inquiry of most Board members. Frequently, the *inexpertise* of members of the board made for thorough and searching consideration of a project to be funded."[15]

One consequence of the method of selecting BMIF board members was that virtually all of the trustees were directly or indirectly connected with agencies that applied for grants from the foundation. One or more of the BMIF trustees were directors or officers of 18 of the 40 agencies that received $100,000 or more in grants from BMIF during 1976-79, the period of its greatest activity. Trustees were also indirectly involved, through spouses or institutional affiliation, in three more of the institutions that received substantial grants. Since the 21 agencies were all conspicuous elements in Columbus's social and cultural life, it is probable that they would have submitted and received grants regardless of BMIF board representation. Trustees scrupulously abstained from voting on requests from agencies in which they were personally involved; some participated in discussions of such requests, while others withheld comment.

The board had decided in February 1976 to require at least four affirmative votes for approval of any grant. In September 1976, on Clark's recommendation, the trustees added the following rule on voting to the foundation's code of regulations:

Regardless of the number of Trustees present and voting at any meeting of the Board of Trustees, the affirmative vote of at least four Trustees shall be required for the approval of any grant of this Foundation. No Trustee who is an officer, principal, trustee or director of any organization applying for a grant from this Foundation shall be entitled to vote on any question relating to such grant.

39

Clark ruled that this regulation disqualified Kessler and Kuhn, both of whom were officers of the Children's Hospital Research Foundation, from voting on a request from that organization, but allowed Mrs. Robert H. Jeffrey, II, the board's United Way representative, whose husband was chairman of the Board of Trustees of Children's Hospital, to vote on the grant. With this precedent, trustees subsequently were able to vote on requests from agencies in which their spouses were involved.

All seven trustees were present at only about one-third of the grant meetings held between 1975 and 1980; six was the average number in attendance, but occasionally there were only five. Once, only four trustees attended. Absences and abstentions sometimes made approvals difficult. When the number of trustees present and eligible to vote on a request was less than four, the trustees present authorized the president to submit a unanimous consent form among all the trustees with the understanding that interested members would abstain from voting. This was done, for example, when an application was received from Goodwill Industries of Central Ohio "to assist in resolving the applicant's current financial crisis" (Minutes, July 11, 1977), or one from United Way of Franklin County for $1 million (December 5, 1977).

In deciding whether to accept or reject the staff recommendation on a given request, BMIF trustees considered matters such as priority of community need for the proposed service or activity, the number and efficacy of similar programs already under way, the ability of the applicant to maintain the operation were a grant awarded, the availability of other funding sources, and the composition of the agency's board of directors. For example, was it a "sweat equity" board that could be counted on for volunteer work, but lacked financial clout, or did it have members with the experience and connections necessary for successful fund-raising? The board and staff did not always agree on these matters, and members of the board occasionally disagreed on issues such as priority of need. Differences of opinion among trustees over major early grants were infrequent; they were not uncommon in respect to relatively small grants for purposes or to agencies whose value and viability were questioned by one or more members of the board.

Support or opposition from a single trustee was sometimes crucial in deciding whether a request would be approved or denied. The board tended to accept a member's favorable judgment on a request in an area in which the trustee was considered expert, as long as the rest of the board felt no serious reservation about the grant. On the other hand, the board might defer to a member's critical assessment and expertise on a request even if the general sentiment was somewhat favorable to the proposal. Questions raised by one or more members sometimes caused postponement of a decision until additional information was submitted. The board denied some requests recognized as worthy either because the agency had already received substantial funds from BMIF, or because if the application were approved, similar unfundable requests would probably be received from a number of other institutions.

Lobbying, whether or not it influenced trustee voting, was a recognized part of the process of awarding grants. When grant seekers asked if they should get in touch with board members, Evans's standard reply was "I can't tell you to, but you would be a fool if you didn't." Conversely, it would have been unwise for the board to have refused applicants a chance to present their cases or to have failed to take community attitudes into consideration. Some lobbying was done informally at dinner parties and other social occasions when friends and fellow guests of trustees discussed the virtues of their agencies and the benefits to be derived from BMIF's generosity. Trustees who represented Capital and Ohio State universities received solicitations directly from grant applicants and indirectly from their respective boards of trustees and administrators. Applicants for small grants ($10,000 to $25,000) lobbied as intensely as those requesting large sums of money. In the case of BMIF's grant to establish Battelle-Darby Creek Metro Park, pressure for approval came not only from the Metropolitan Park District of Columbus and Franklin County, but also from business and financial interests that strongly favored the grant.

Aside from its two representatives on the Board of Trustees, Battelle Memorial Institute refrained from efforts to influence board or staff decisions. The only occasion on which BMIF officially asked the institute's advice was in connection with two proactive gifts, both made in September 1979. These were grants made to the Pacific Science Center Foundation and the University of Washington in recognition of the contribution BMI facilities and operations in Richland and Seattle had made to the foundation's assets. Heffner and Batch, and later, Heffner and Ungar, the BMI representatives, did not vote as a bloc and, in fact, sometimes voted on opposite sides. However, the foundation's trustees were committed to memorializing the name of Gordon Battelle and, by prompt and responsible disposal of the foundation's endowment, to enhancing the image of Battelle Memorial Institute.

To the general public, the distinction between BMIF and BMI was never clear. Therefore, most people assumed that the "Battelle" in the Battelle Scholars Program, the Battelle Human Resources Building, and the Battelle-Darby Creek Metro Park signified the Battelle Memorial Institute, not Gordon Battelle or the Battelle Foundation.

Major Grant Decisions

Basic decisions about BMIF's policies and operations were made at the time of its organization. The articles of incorporation prohibited grants to private individuals or for purposes that would adversely affect the corporation's tax-exempt status. The articles also required distribution in each calendar year of at least six percent of BMIF's assets. Both the code of regulations and deed of gift prohibited grants to BMI, affiliates, or organizations it controlled. The deed of gift required that all net income from the founding contribution be distributed annually and declared that grants should be "substantially limited" to those benefiting central Ohio. It also limited BMIF's distributions to education, scientific research, and programs to improve the quality of life.

Subject to these rules, BMIF trustees had discretion not only to determine the beneficiary and amount of individual awards, but also to establish overall policies. These policies included the annual rate of distribution, the division of funds among the foundation's areas of interest, the types of activities to be aided, the extent to which matching grants should be used, and the apportionment of grants between Columbus and other areas of central Ohio. Some of these issues had been discussed at the October 20, 1975, meeting, when the board made certain broad policy decisions. At that time, the trustees set $1 million as a maximum and $10,000 as a normal minimum for individual grants, projected distribution of no more than $1 million by March 1976, and estimated annual distribution thereafter at the rate of about $3 million a year.

Once in operation, BMIF awarded grants that were both larger and smaller than anticipated. The two largest grants were awards of $2 million to establish the Battelle Scholars Program and $1.5 million to the Children's Hospital Research Foundation, both approved in 1976. Between December 1975 and July 1981, the foundation awarded 30 grants for $10,000 or less and eight grants for $5,000 or less. More important, BMIF distributed the major part of its funds more rapidly than expected. In each of the first two years of awarding grants, the amount awarded exceeded $6 million, and in the third year, 1977-78, it approached $4 million. Almost two-thirds of the grants awarded between December 1975 and July 1981, and more than three-fourths of the $21.9 million distributed in that period, had been allocated before October 31, 1978.

Although the board agreed that "BMIF wants to 'make things happen' that otherwise would not come to pass," and, therefore, favored large or at least substantial grants, the board was often reminded of what

Heffner called "the many small activities that help." Applications varied widely in the amounts requested, and BMIF's awards also covered a broad range. Of the 175 awards granted between 1975 and 1981, 13 were for $500,000 or more, 53 for more than $74,000 but less than $500,000, 53 for more than $20,000 but less than $75,000, and 56 for $20,000 or less. The median grant for the five and a half-year period was $35,000; the average grant was $125,000. Because the board had decided to complete distribution in a relatively short period, BMIF's grants were greater in size than those of other foundations with comparable or even much larger assets.[16] The following table indicates the volume and range of grants awarded in each year of BMIF's history.[17]

			Grants			
Year	President	Awarded	High	Low	Median	Total
1975-76	Heffner	51	$1,500,000	$6,000	$ 37,500	$6,040,072
1976-77	Kessler	25	2,000,000	1,200	100,000	6,545,792
1977-78	Langevin	28	1,000,000	5,000	35,000	3,922,325
1978-79	Petropoulos	29	200,000	1,000	50,000	1,680,472
1979-80	Ungar	21	500,000	5,000	39,160	1,345,138
1980-81	Stegemoeller	21	675,000	6,000	50,000	2,378,000
Total						$21,911,799

Each presidential year had its distinctive style in grant decisions. During Heffner's administration, the board acted on the largest number of applications (200), approved the largest number of grants, and established BMIF's pattern of heavy investment in capital improvements and responsiveness to social welfare agencies. Among the major grants awarded were $1.5 million to the Children's Hospital Research Foundation as an endowment for pediatric medical research; $500,000 to the Columbus Association for the Performing Arts for improvements in the Ohio Theatre; $373,000 to the Columbus College of Art and Design for purchase, remodeling, and repair of facilities; and $600,000 to the Columbus Board of Education for building, renovation, and equipment at the Ft. Hayes Career Center.

Kessler's term as president saw the second heaviest load of applications; it was also a period of large grants to establish the Battelle Scholars Program and Battelle-Darby Creek Metro Park and to the Columbus Museum of Art, Center of Science and Industry, and Jewish Center. Fewer than half as many applications were approved in 1976-77 as in 1975-76, but because of the number of large awards, the median grant was $100,000, the highest in BMIF's history. Four grants that totaled slightly more than $100,000 went to organizations seeking peaceful implementation of the Columbus school desegregation plan.

During 1977-78, when Langevin was president, BMIF focused attention on the arts, an area in which some grants had been postponed until the Cultural Explorations study had been completed. The Columbus Symphony Orchestra, Players Club Foundation, and Ballet Metropolitan were among the recipients of large grants. In 1978, BMIF also gave United Way of Franklin County $1 million for purchase of the Battelle Human Services Building.

Under Petropoulos and his successors, Ungar and Stegemoeller, BMIF faced the problem of making significant and innovative grants at a time when the foundation's resources were much more limited than during its first three years. In 1978-79, applications fell below 100 for the first time, but the percentage approved was the highest. Thirty percent of that year's applications were approved, and the size of the median grant was the second highest in BMIF's history. Half of the grants that year went to educational institutions or projects. These included scholarships to allow young people from minority and lower- and middle-income families to attend the Columbus Academy and Columbus School for Girls and to recruit and train volunteers to teach language skills to functionally illiterate adults. The largest grant went to The Ohio State University Development Fund for the benefit of the university's Telecommunications Center. The number of applications and approvals declined in 1979-80. Grants were made to 13 social welfare and health agencies and for a riverfront park in downtown Columbus, a pharmacology/toxicology center at Children's Hospital, establishment of the Kenyon Repertory Theater, and for assistance to the supplemental campaign of United Way of Franklin County. Many applications were made in 1980-81, as hopeful agencies tried to meet the December 1980 deadline for final receipt of grant proposals. A major factor in BMIF's response to applications in both 1979-80 and 1980-81 was the board's determination to reserve part of the foundation's remaining funds for proactive giving. The next section discusses the processes involved in BMIF's final grant decisions.

BMI's deed of gift specified the methods and the objects of the distribution and recommended using challenge grants and giving in ways that would encourage, rather than discourage, charitable donations by others. At the October 20, 1975, meeting, the trustees agreed that in making awards, the foundation would normally use the matching device. Very early in BMIF's operations, however, it became clear that in a community such as Columbus, this device had to be used carefully. In a memorandum accompanying the docket for BMIF's first grant meeting, Richard Oman made the following observation: "There is always a limit on the ability of local funding sources at any given time to provide the necessary money for new buildings or major improvements to physical plants of philanthropic agencies." Six of the 31 grants awarded at the first two grant meetings called for matches totaling $378,000. Although the sum was not excessive, both board members and community leaders recognized that overuse of the matching device by BMIF might put unusual demands on corporations and individual donors in Columbus. A staff report on a proposal for $1 million from BMIF to be matched by a like amount from other sources contained this comment: "Some resistance exists in the community to the type of pressure that results from this type of grant."[18] After May 1976, the board tried to schedule its challenge grants so as to avoid too much matching activity at any one time.

BMIF grant agreements sometimes contained restrictions on fund-raising efforts of grantees. The agreement in the foundation's 1976 matching grant to the Columbus Public Schools for the Ft. Hayes Career Center included this statement: "The grantee is urged to refrain from actively seeking such matching funds from private sources in Franklin County." In a case involving a proposed matching grant to an agency located in Knox County, the BMIF staff recommended that matching funds should be obtained "from outside Franklin and contiguous counties." The board then approved a grant "contingent on a match outside Franklin County."[19] Contingencies in matching grants included a date—often the end of the calendar year in which the grant was made—at which time the matching funds had to be secured. In some cases, BMIF grants provided the local match required for a grant from a federal agency; in others, as in grants to the Capitol South Association and Columbus Department of Recreation and Parks, BMIF's awards were contingent upon the grantees receiving anticipated funds from government agencies. The Survey of Recipients estimated that about $11.3 million was raised from other sources by agencies that received BMIF grants before October 31, 1979. No grant was rescinded because the required matching funds could not be obtained.

BMIF, like other private foundations, had to operate within the parameters fixed by the Tax Reform Act of 1969. The law subjected foundations to complex regulations and imposed sanctions for prohibited actions and for failure to meet reporting, payout, and other technical requirements. At the time the law was enacted, it was believed to curtail foundation activities drastically. By 1975, when BMIF came into

45

existence, the Council on Foundations was advising its members that the requirements of the law and Treasury Department regulations were not as rigorous as was at first assumed. It reported that foundations could still be adventurous and make grants to individuals, to donees other than established public charities, and to groups without tax-exempt status if certain requirements were met.[20]

BMIF, itself the product of a legal controversy, adopted and maintained a cautious policy on legal and fiscal matters. The Board of Trustees closely followed the advice of legal counsel not only on questions of voting or abstaining, but also on interpretations of "self-dealing," "disqualified persons," and "qualifying distribution." William Clark reviewed applications received by the foundation and proposed board actions on other matters to alert trustees of possible objections from the Internal Revenue Service. He reminded trustees that BMIF must exercise expenditure responsibility (i.e., require a final financial report showing how grant funds were expended) when the receiver or user of the grant did not have tax-exempt status. He stipulated that the proper disclaimer must be included in grant agreements so that a BMIF award would not endanger the tax status of agencies classified as public charities.

BMIF's distribution was confined almost exclusively to agencies that had received tax-exempt status and for which the foundation did not have to exercise expenditure responsibility. "If the grantee qualifies as a public charity and the purpose of the grant falls within the scope of its charitable activities," Clark advised the trustees in 1977, "the Foundation may assume that the grant proceeds will be applied for that purpose and need not verify that fact after the grant has been made."[21] Limiting grants to agencies that had received 501(c)(3) status simplified BMIF operations, but had the effect of restricting the foundation's awards to "safe," noncontroversial causes.

Because most BMIF grants represented substantial sums of money, grant decisions had to take into consideration the managerial strength or weakness of the agencies that requested assistance as well as the prospective donee's ability or inability to use the funds effectively and responsibly. These were matters on which there could be differences of opinion, but as a general rule, BMIF grants went to strong and well-established agencies rather than to weak and struggling ones. The following table lists the ten agencies receiving the largest sums from BMIF. The $10.5 million received by these agencies represented 47.9 percent of BMIF's total distribution.

Many factors influenced BMIF grant policies and determined the rate, directions, and characteristics of their distribution. The most important consideration in shaping grant decisions, however, was trustee obligation

Agencies Receiving Largest Sums

Rank	Agency	Total Received from BMIF
1	Children's Hospital Research Foundation	$ 1,608,576
2	United Way of Franklin County	1,325,000
3	The Ohio State University (including OSU Research Foundation)	1,154,000
4	Columbus Public Schools (plus $78,750 interest on $525,000)	1,139,246
5	City of Columbus	1,020,000
6	Columbus Symphony Orchestra	1,000,000
7	Metropolitan Park District of Columbus and Franklin County	1,000,000
8	Columbus Museum of Art	841,758
9	Columbus Association for the Performing Arts	751,000
10	Center of Science and Industry	684,182
Total		$10,523,762

to carry out responsibilities in accordance with prudent business principles and in a way that would enhance the reputation of BMI and its founder.

Winding Up

Because BMIF's charge and intent were to distribute virtually all of the founding contribution in a period of five to ten years, questions of how and when to dissolve the foundation were discussed early in its history. The board's first discussion of dissolution took place toward the end of BMIF's second grant year. In October 1977, when about two-thirds of the founding contribution had been distributed, the board agreed to maintain existing policies, but to proceed with caution in regard to future funding. On July 28, 1978, the officers (Langevin, president; Kuhn, secretary; Petropoulos, treasurer; and Evans, executive director) considered the possibility of reducing grant levels and eliminating one staff position as a result of BMIF's dwindling fund balance.

The full Board of Trustees, in approving the budget for 1979, in December 1978 retained both professional staff positions, but reduced the authorized level of spending for accounting, legal, and public relations services. In November 1978, the trustees decided to award an average of $410,000 at each quarterly meeting during 1979 and 1980 and to end the grant program in December 1980. Since the amounts awarded in

James I. Luck
Executive Director
1980-82

Pamela S. Faccinto
Executive Secretary
1980-82

1979 were lower than anticipated, the trustees, in March 1980, postponed final awards and close of operations until 1981. They set December 31, 1980, as the final date for receiving applications.

During the last two years of BMIF's existence, changes occurred in both board and staff membership. In the summer of 1979 Ann Reynolds and Harvey Stegemoeller replaced Kuhn and Langevin as representatives of The Ohio State University Research Foundation and Capital University. Ellen Gruber, administrative officer, and Bruce Evans, executive director, resigned in 1979. James I. Luck succeeded Evans in January 1980. Luck had a diverse background, including serving as director of forensics at Texas Christian University, executive director of the National Congress on Volunteerism and Citizenship, and a fellow in public management at the Academy for Contemporary Problems.

Continuity, not change, was the purpose of a 1980 amendment of BMIF's articles of incorporation and code of regulations that allowed Robert H. Potts to continue as United Way representative on BMIF's Board of Trustees during the phase-out period.

Assuring continuation of the Battelle Scholars Program was a subject of major concern in all discussions of dissolution plans. How to dispose of the fund earmarked for administration of the program, originally $125,000 but raised to $200,000 in November 1978, was identified as a problem. A second problem that surfaced was the questionable adequacy of the scholarships in view of increasing college tuition and room and board costs. In September 1980, the board agreed that a trust should be established for the specific purpose of administering the Battelle Scholars Program after BMIF's dissolution and that funds remaining with or reverting to BMIF after dissolution should be assigned to the Battelle Scholars Program Trust. The second problem was resolved in October 1980 when the trustees decided to reserve $638,000 of the foundation's funds for supplemental grants to the eight central Ohio colleges and universities participating in the program. This would permit increases in awards to $2,000 per year at Ohio State and Franklin universities, and $4,000 per year at the remaining private institutions. In March 1981, the board accepted a draft trust agreement prepared by counsel for BMIF for consideration by participating institutions. The revised trust agreement, incorporating changes to meet questions raised by some of the college administrations, was approved by the board on June 1, 1981.

The agreement established the Battelle Scholars Program Trust Fund to assume the responsibility BMIF had exercised over monitoring and administering the program. Any funds that reverted to BMIF or became payable to it after BMIF's dissolution would be received by the trust fund and would be distributed to the participating colleges and universities in proportion to the number of full-time equivalent students attending each institution. A provision was included that ensured no single institution would receive more than one-third of the total amount distributed. The trust fund was to be governed by three trustees, one representing BMI and serving an indefinite term and two appointed by the participating colleges and universities on an alphabetical basis to serve for two-year rotating terms. The agreement did not stipulate the number or amount of awards to be offered, but authorized each institution to use income from the Battelle Scholars Program endowments to award scholarships ranging from 50 to 100 percent of the annual charge for tuition. Residence in central Ohio and potential for leadership remained the prime requirements for selection. The trust agreement also provided for amendments to, or termination of, the program should changing circumstances in higher education or the participating institutions make such action necessary. In that event, distribution of the trust's assets would be on the basis of full-time equivalent students at each institution.

In June 1981, the board also approved supplemental grants totaling $675,000 to eight Battelle Scholars Program endowments in central Ohio and a supplemental grant of $25,000 to the Battelle Scholars Program at the University of Washington, Richland. The supplements amounted to one-third of the original endowments except in the case of Ohio Wesleyan and Franklin universities, which received slightly more than one-third.

A nnouncement of the December 31, 1980, deadline for the receipt of applications brought the largest number of requests since 1975. During the last quarter of 1980, 103 agencies requested amounts ranging from as little as $1,861 to a high of $1 million. They totaled $11.5 million. Since BMIF had only about $1.5 million in uncommitted funds at the end of 1980, it was apparent that only a few of the requests could be funded. In reviewing the applications, Luck considered the purpose and the amount of the request in the light of previous applications and earlier grants, the agency's plans for long-term support, and the possible significance or impact of the proposed award. He recommended denial of many applications with summary review.

The board was no less rigorous than Luck, denying 43 and postponing two of the 55 proposals listed on the dockets for the March and June 1981 grant meetings. Only ten agencies survived the elimination process, and only three received the amounts they had requested.

BMIF's response to these and the other applications received in its last two years of operations was conditioned by the board's commitment to apply a large portion of the funds remaining to proactive gifts. Instead of allowing the foundation's resources to be spent gradually on projects similar to those already supported, the board sought to identify new areas of need where reasonably large grants could make a significant impact on Columbus and the central Ohio community. The ability to evaluate proactive grants was one of the criteria used in rating candidates interviewed as possible replacements for Bruce Evans.

At the December 1979 board meeting, Evans, the outgoing executive director, suggested several grant ideas that included establishing an endowment for guest artists and humanists and expansion of the Ohio Theatre to provide office and rehearsal space for arts organizations. In March 1980, Luck presented a set of criteria for evaluating and generating proactive grant ideas and suggested two additional proactive grant possibilities: an endowment for educational enrichment of disadvantaged children and a riverfront park in the proposed Columbus Civic Center. The trustees directed Luck to confer with civic leaders and prepare a full range of proactive possibilities. Luck's report, presented in June 1980, also used responses to a question on this history project's survey of BMIF grant recipients: "If you had $2 million to invest in a grant or grants for the Columbus community, how would you distribute the funds?"

The list compiled by Luck contained 14 possibilities—two in the arts, six relating to Columbus Public Schools, two each in higher education (including expansion of the Battelle Scholars Program) and social services, a fund for encouraging and rewarding excellence in the community through annual awards of Battelle Prizes, and the development of a civic center park. During the summer of 1980, the trustees ranked the proposals according to their degree of importance and likelihood of success with and without BMIF support. The projects that received the most favorable response from the board were expansion of the Battelle Scholars Program, programs to strengthen the Columbus Public Schools, and the civic center park. As mentioned above, the trustees approved expansion of the Battelle Scholars Program in principle in October 1980 and funded the supplemental endowments in June 1981. The other proactive projects are discussed in order of their approval by the board.

BMIF's interest in riverfront beautification and downtown development led the Columbus Department of Recreation and Parks to request $1 million in matching assistance to construct a civic center park. The board considered this request in June and September 1980, but took no action at that time. In October 1980, it approved a grant of $500,000 as a challenge or "last dollar" grant contingent on the department's raising the additional $5,175,000 needed to complete the park by February 28, 1981. Subsequently, the board extended the deadline to allow the department more time to obtain additional support. In June 1981, after the city of Columbus had committed $1 million to the undertaking, the board released $500,000 to provide last dollar funds to create a $1.5 million version of the project to be known as Battelle Riverfront Park.

In considering the ways BMIF might "give a real boost," in the words of one trustee, to secondary education and to demonstrate its concern for public education in Columbus, the board examined the possibility of providing proactive grants to establish a science school, scholarships for high school graduates, and a program for gifted and talented students. After preliminary discussion work by the late Jack Gibbs and with school officials, a plan was developed to establish a resource center for gifted and talented science and mathematics students at the Ft. Hayes Career Center. Luck made the following statement in a letter inviting Columbus's education, business, and foundation leaders to participate in a meeting to examine the plan:

> Columbus is home to nationally significant scientific, high technology, research and educational institutions. This creates an opportunity to enrich the public educational program in relevant fields of learning. Thus, an accelerated math and science program for upper level, gifted and talented students makes good sense. . . .
>
> The Columbus Public Schools offer performing arts programs at Ft. Hayes that attract students from Worthington, Bexley and other suburban districts. To create course offerings in the core curriculum areas (such as math and science) that would be attractive in the same way would make a strong, positive statement about educational quality. The potential for increased public support and further positive steps are manifest.[22]

The meeting, held on February 25, 1981, led to the formation of a ten-member task force that met on March 17, 1981, to clarify the scope and structure of the program. On the basis of agreements reached at the task force meeting, Howard Merriman, assistant superintendent of the Columbus Public Schools, prepared a prospectus for a science and mathematics resource center for gifted students, and on April 10, 1981, the Columbus Public Schools submitted a revised request to BMIF for funding to establish the center. The board considered the request at its June 1981 meeting and asked for more information regarding implementation of the proposal.

Among other proactive grant areas in which the board expressed interest were teacher awards and measures to combat adolescent drug and

Battelle Youth Science Program, Columbus Public Schools

alcohol abuse. In March 1981, Luck recommended, and the board approved, a grant of $10,000 to the Franklin County Teacher Center for a one-year program of awards. The grants provided gifts of up to $500 for excellence in teaching and were awarded to individuals selected from the 4,500 teachers in 17 public and private school districts in Franklin County outside of the Columbus Public Schools. In June, the board accepted Luck's recommendation that the foundation grant $50,000 to help the Columbus Area Council on Alcoholism implement its program, Chemical Intervention: A Youth Support Network. The program called for formation of parent/family and community support groups; development of school programs and policies on substance abuse; training of teachers, parents, and students; and heightening of public awareness of drug and alcohol abuse among adolescents.

The board held a special meeting on July 2, 1981, and made what was anticipated to be its final grants. The largest sum was $525,000 given to the Columbus Public Schools to endow the faculty for a science and mathematics resource center for gifted and talented students (including accumulated interest, the amount distributed was $603,750). This grant, which fulfilled the board's objective to make a meaningful contribution to improve the academic quality of public education in Columbus, included a set of special conditions intended to ensure continued emphasis on excellence in the operation of the program. To balance the award to the Columbus Public Schools, an award of $78,000 was made to The Ohio State University Research Foundation to develop a remedial mathematics course for underprepared high school seniors who planned to attend college. A grant of $100,000 to the Columbus Museum of Art completed BMIF's gifts to the arts and humanities. Awards of $50,000 to the city of Columbus and $225,000 to the Columbus Department of Recreation and Parks exemplified the partnership of private philanthropy and public agencies that was characteristic of BMIF's efforts in the area of civic betterment.

Completing the awarding of grants did not end the operation of BMIF. A number of activities continued, including executing grant agreements, monitoring the drug and alcohol abuse grant, planning for the science and mathematics resource center, obtaining final expenditure reports from grantees, preparing and executing necessary amendments, and arranging for receipt of unexpended grants or those reverting to BMIF. All of these activities had to be completed before the foundation could be dissolved. Other activities to be completed prior to dissolution included preparation of the 1980-81 annual report, compilation of a summary of BMIF's operations for distribution at the time of dissolution, and a review of an independently produced history and evaluation of BMIF.

Two developments in particular affected the timing of BMIF's close-out: creation of the Battelle Scholars Program Trust Fund and disbursement of BMIF's grant to the Columbus Public Schools for the Gifted and Talented Science and Mathematics Resource Center. The former involved approval of the trust by the Internal Revenue Service and ratification by BMI and the participating colleges and universities of the trust agreement, scholarship amendment, supplemental grant agreement, and distribution of supplemental grants. This action was completed in various stages between August 1981 and July 1982. On June 17, 1982, a special governing committee appointed by BMIF approved plans developed by the school system in accordance with conditions set forth by the Gifted and Talented Science and Mathematics Resource Center grant agreement, and $603,750 was disbursed to endow the faculty of the center.

On June 22, 1982, the BMIF trustees met for the final time. Luck was designated to handle dissolution and all remaining BMIF activities. A grant of $200,000 was approved to the Battelle Scholars Program Trust Fund. Remaining furniture and equipment were also assigned to the trust fund.

Funds remaining on July 30, 1982, were designated for transfer to The Columbus Foundation. As executive director of that foundation, Luck would make certain that BMIF's legal, accounting, excise tax, and other obligations would be met. The board assigned Luck the responsibility for arranging the editing, publication, and distribution of the history. In their final act, the BMIF trustees approved July 30, 1982, as the date for dissolution.

NOTES AND SOURCES

Notes

1. Sherwood L. Fawcett to John W. Gardner, January 17, 1975, BMIF Correspondence Files, Requests to Participate.

2. "Prospectus for the Trustees of the Battelle Memorial Institute Foundation," May 1975, BMIF History Project Files, Basic Documents.

3. "Articles of Incorporation of Battelle Memorial Institute Foundation," BMIF Correspondence Files, Battelle Memorial Institute Foundation.

4. "Agreement Deed of Gift," July 7, 1975, BMIF Minutes, June 3 to October 31, 1976.

5. In addition to $15.4 million called for in the agreement of May 7, 1975, the founding contribution included $3.5 million in mortgage notes of Children's Hospital, Columbus.

6. BMIF Correspondence Files, Merrimon Cuninggim, Consultant.

7. Cuninggim's report is filed with BMIF Minutes, August 26, 1975.

8. BMIF Correspondence Files, BMIF—Fourth Board of Trustees Meeting—October 20, 1975, and October 20 Meeting Questionnaires and Results.

   The policy against grants for religious purposes was similar to, and inspired by, the prohibition of distributions for religious or political purposes in Section 6.1.2 of BMI's corporate policy manual. See memorandum from G. C. Heffner to James I. Luck, March 25, 1981, BMIF Correspondence Files, Thomas H. Langevin and Associates.

9. G. C. Heffner to BMIF Trustees, September 11, 1975, BMIF Correspondence Files, October 20 Meeting Questionnaires and Results.

10. William S. Guthrie to Sherwood L. Fawcett, May 23, 1975, BMIF Correspondence Files, The Columbus Foundation.

11. Richard H. Oman, Leeda Marting, and Elizabeth Deinhardt to the Trustees of the Battelle Memorial Institute Foundation, November 24, 1975, The Columbus Foundation Correspondence Files, Battelle Memorial Institute Foundation.

12. Criteria and qualifications for additional staff person to be hired by the Battelle Memorial Institute Foundation, BMIF Correspondence Files, Program Coordinator.

13. Albert J. Kuhn and Thomas H. Langevin, Battelle Memorial Institute Foundation: "Initiatives in Leadership for Tomorrow," Board Minutes, November 1, 1976.

14. "The Grant-making Process" (mimeographed form included in case folders).

15. Memorandum from Albert J. Kuhn to James I. Luck, undated (March/April 1981), Langevin Associates File.

16. American Association of Fund-Raising Counsel, Inc., *Giving USA,* 26th Annual Issue (New York: 1981), p. 15.

17. In the winding down stage, the initiating president (Heffner) was also the foundation's final president (1981-82). During this period, additional funds distributed were $78,750, the interest accrued on the Columbus Public Schools grant of $525,000, and $200,000 to the Battelle Scholars Program. From the time the Battelle Scholars Program Endowment was established in 1977, until its distribution to the Battelle Scholars Program Trust Fund in 1982, net earnings were $36,878. These distributions brought total grant awards to $22,227,427.

18. BMIF Case File 281.

19. BMIF Case File 743.

20. Jack Shakely, "Tom Troyer Appraises the Tax Reform Act of 1969," *Foundation News,* May-June 1980, p. 24.

21. Memorandum from William L. Clark to G. C. Heffner, June 2, 1977, BMIF Correspondence Files, Knepper, White, Arter & Hadden.

22. Luck's letter, dated February 13, 1981, and the list of persons to whom it was addressed are in BMIF Case File 855.

Sources

Part 1—Background and Organization:

BMIF Legal Proceedings Folder.

BMIF Minutes, June 3, July 7, August 26, and October 20, 1975.

"Report to the Trustees," BMIF, Merrimon Cuninggim, August 26, 1975.

BMIF Correspondence Files:
  BMIF Budget
  BMIF—Request to Participate
  Board Member Selection
  BMIF—Fourth Board of Trustees Meeting—October 20, 1975
  October 20 Meeting Questionnaires and Results
  Public Relations
  Thomas H. Langevin and Associates

Interviews:

  G. C. Heffner, assistant to the president, Battelle Memorial Institute, Columbus, Ohio, June 5, 1980

  Sherwood L. Fawcett, president, Battelle Memorial Institute, Columbus, Ohio, November 4, 1980

Part 2—Getting Under Way, 1975-76:

BMIF Minutes, October 20, 1975, to December 6, 1976.
BMIF Correspondence Files:
  Arts Policy
  Battelle Memorial Institute Foundation
  Battelle Scholars Program

The Columbus Foundation
Council on Foundations, 1975-76
Program Coordinator

The Columbus Foundation Correspondence Files:
Battelle Memorial Institute Foundation

Part 3—Process of Awarding Grants:

BMIF Board Minutes.

BMIF Case Files.

BMIF Correspondence Files:
Battelle Memorial Institute
The Columbus Foundation
"The Grant-making Process" (mimeographed form included in most case files)
Memorandum from Thomas H. Langevin to Robert H. Bremner, November 11, 1980

Interviews:

Albert Kuhn, professor, The Ohio State University, Columbus, Ohio, May 29, 1980

Richard Oman, attorney at law, Porter, Wright, Morris & Arthur, Columbus, Ohio, June 3, 1980

G. C. Heffner, assistant to the president, Battelle Memorial Institute, Columbus, Ohio, June 5, 1980

Elizabeth Deinhardt, former staff member, The Columbus Foundation, Columbus, Ohio, June 6, 1980

Leeda Marting, executive director, John Hay Whitney Foundation, Columbus, Ohio, June 17, 1980

James Petropoulos, BMIF board member, Columbus, Ohio, June 19, 1980

Ann Reynolds, BMIF board member, Columbus, Ohio, June 27, 1980

W. Bruce Evans, vice president for development, Franklin University, Columbus, Ohio, October 8, 1980

Sherwood L. Fawcett, president, Battelle Memorial Institute, Columbus, Ohio, November 4, 1980

James I. Luck, executive director, Battelle Memorial Institute Foundation, Columbus, Ohio, January 14 and 27, 1981

Part 4—Major Grant Decisions:

BMIF Board Minutes.

BMIF Case Files.

Stanley S. Weithorn, "Summary of Tax Reform Act as It Affects Foundations," *Foundation News,* May-June 1970, pp. 85-89.

Memorandum from Thomas H. Langevin to Robert H. Bremner, January 7, 1981.

Interviews:

Richard Oman, attorney at law, Porter, Wright, Morris & Arthur, Columbus, Ohio, June 3, 1980

G. C. Heffner, assistant to the president, Battelle Memorial Institute, Columbus, Ohio, June 5, 1980

James I. Luck, executive director, Battelle Memorial Institute Foundation, Columbus, Ohio, July 24, 1981

Edward W. Ungar, BMIF board member, Columbus, Ohio, October 8, 1981

Part 5—Winding Up:

BMIF Board Minutes.

BMIF Docket Books, December 3, 1979, to September 30, 1981.

BMIF Case Files.

BMIF Proactive Files:
  Battelle Riverfront Park
  Future of Battelle Scholars
  Education
  Teacher Awards
  Miscellaneous
  Gifted and Talented Program
  Questionnaire
  Battelle Prize
  Consortium of Colleges and Universities
  Ohio Theatre

Interviews:

James I. Luck, executive director, Battelle Memorial Institute Foundation, Columbus, Ohio, July 24 and October 8, 1981

Edward W. Ungar, BMIF board member, Columbus, Ohio, October 1, 1981

Howard Merriman, assistant superintendent, Columbus Public Schools, Columbus, Ohio, October 13, 1981 (telephone)

Terry Roark, associate provost, The Ohio State University, Columbus, Ohio, October 14, 1981

Harvey Stegemoeller, BMIF board member, Columbus, Ohio, October 19, 1981

"Community leaders unanimously agreed that BMIF came at just the right time for Columbus"

CHAPTER III

The Impact of BMIF Grants

From December 1975 through September 1981, BMIF made 175 grants totaling $21,911, 799.[1] An additional grant of $200,000 to the Battelle Scholars Program Trust was approved on June 22, 1982. The funds set aside for the Battelle Scholars Program Endowment in an earlier grant and a grant for the Columbus Public Schools math and science program earned $115,628 prior to distribution. Payment of the additional $315,628 in grants brings the total grants paid by the foundation to $22,227,427. Distribution by type of institution or agency funded was as shown in the table on the following page (also see Figure 1).

The kinds of activities supported are shown by percentage of grants and dollars in Figure 2. Capital improvement was the activity supported by the largest percentage of BMIF grants (36 percent) and the major share of its dollars (46 percent). In dollars, endowment represented the next largest share (33 percent). Special programs and program development ranked next to capital improvement in number of grants.

Grants by Type of Institution

Type of Institution	Number of Grants	Dollars	Percentage
Educational	25	$5,768,049	26
Social Services	61	5,577,456	26
Civic (including government and historical and scientific museums)	47	4,318,737	20
Arts and Humanities	24	3,540,758	16
Health and Medical	19	2,706,799	12

The nature of community benefit is shown also by percentage of grants and dollars in Figure 3. Almost one-third of BMIF's grants benefited community social service, but these tended to be smaller in dollar amount than those benefiting education. Slightly more than half of BMIF's dollar distribution went in nearly equal shares toward improving educational opportunity and quality (29 percent) and social service programs and facilities (26 percent).

BMIF's distribution both resembled and differed from the general pattern of foundation giving in the United States during the period of its operation. The foundation distributed about the same share of its funds to education and welfare as the national average. It gave slightly more than the national average (13.6 percent) to arts and humanities and considerably less than the national average (22.6 percent and 11.6 percent) to health and science.[2]

In an effort to evaluate BMIF as fully as possible, a number of other activities were carried out. These included a determination of the opinions of selected community leaders through interviews, a collection and analysis of the opinions and factual reports of grant recipients, a collection of data and interviews with officials of some agencies that were not successful in obtaining a grant, and the establishment of a coding system for perceiving or analyzing the characteristics of grants.

In soliciting opinions of community leaders and grant recipients, questions of impact often related to respondent impressions of the BMIF board itself. Hence, in the accounts that follow, there are opinions of how well the BMIF board carried out its responsibility, as well as how its grants affected the community. The distinction is not always clear since an individual's opinion of the board is often a reflection of that individual's opinion of the success of the grants themselves.

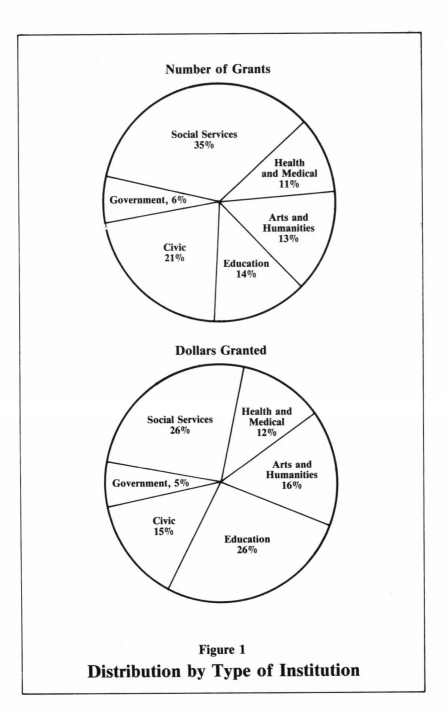

Number of Grants

Social Services 35%

Health and Medical 11%

Government, 6%

Arts and Humanities 13%

Civic 21%

Education 14%

Dollars Granted

Social Services 26%

Health and Medical 12%

Government, 5%

Arts and Humanities 16%

Civic 15%

Education 26%

Figure 1
Distribution by Type of Institution

Community Reactions

When the BMIF board sought its early directions, as described earlier, it secured the counsel of Merrimon Cuninggim. The advice Cuninggim gave the trustees was based, in part, on expectations for the foundation held by various community leaders he interviewed. A similar interview approach was adopted in this history as a way to evaluate how well the foundation performed its tasks. The theme of these "post-BMIF" interviews was leader opinions of BMIF achievements as they compared to expectations when the foundation began. All of the interviews that form the basis of the following description were conducted from November 1980 to January 1981. The 14 individuals interviewed included some of those contacted by Cuninggim as well as others selected because of their prominence in and sensitivity to community affairs.[3]

Community leaders unanimously agreed that BMIF came at just the right time for Columbus. All those interviewed mentioned the receptivity of central Ohio to such a funding effort. One thought of Columbus as an active "seed bed." Another saw the BMIF efforts as "fertilization" in rich soil. As indicated below, some negative feelings were voiced about specific issues, but there were no general negative impressions in any one of the interviews.

Interviewees were encouraged to express themselves freely, rather than react to specific questions or statements. Taken together, the interviews produced a number of key factors:

1. *Timing/tempo.* There was general agreement that the foundation board acted wisely in distributing the funds in a relatively short time, so that momentum was established in the community.

2. *Size of grants.* While two people felt not enough attention was given to small grants, all of those interviewed felt the foundation board was wise to emphasize grants sizable enough to make a difference.

3. *Makeup of board.* Several people felt the board was not representative of central Ohio. One stressed the lack of minority representation, while another saw it as geographically limited. This was a reservation Cuninggim had expressed earlier. Those who held that opinion, however, joined with the others interviewed in noting that the membership of the board represented the influence, power, and ability to take action quickly. This underlined the general impression that quick distribution of the BMIF funds was in the public interest. The attitude implicit in these comments was that even if there was a lack of complete representation on the board, it had carried out a very broad-based program.

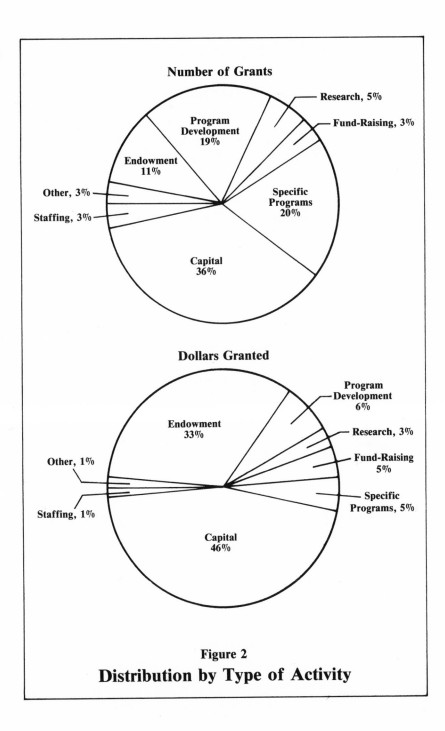

Number of Grants

Research, 5%

Fund-Raising, 3%

Program Development 19%

Endowment 11%

Other, 3%

Staffing, 3%

Specific Programs 20%

Capital 36%

Dollars Granted

Program Development 6%

Research, 3%

Fund-Raising 5%

Endowment 33%

Other, 1%

Staffing, 1%

Specific Programs, 5%

Capital 46%

Figure 2

Distribution by Type of Activity

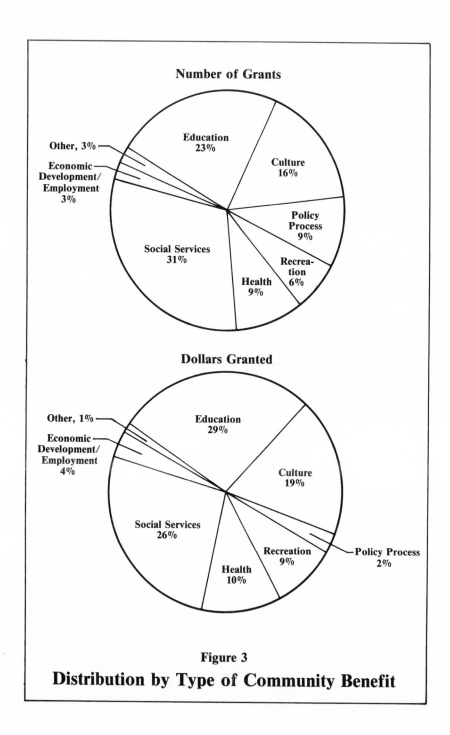

Number of Grants

Education 23%

Other, 3%

Economic Development/ Employment 3%

Culture 16%

Policy Process 9%

Social Services 31%

Recreation 6%

Health 9%

Dollars Granted

Other, 1%

Economic Development/ Employment 4%

Education 29%

Culture 19%

Social Services 26%

Recreation 9%

Policy Process 2%

Health 10%

Figure 3

Distribution by Type of Community Benefit

4. *Board policy.* The impression of those interviewed was that the board acted conservatively, funding institutions that were stable and reputable. There was agreement that high-risk situations were not compatible with the nature and timing of the foundation efforts and that the board's reliance upon stability was in keeping with the expectation of the community.

5. *Matching grants.* Board policy and actions on matching grants received favorable comment in the interviews. Every interviewee making a statement on the subject felt positively about BMIF's sensitivity to the danger of too many campaigns in the community at one time while, at the same time, encouraging the appropriate use of the matching funds concept. Everyone interviewed felt that charity *had* been significantly advanced in central Ohio, and most felt BMIF would have some enduring effect on philanthropy in the area. Only one thought that there would be no enduring charitable impulse resulting from BMIF involvement.

6. *Board/staff behavior.* In every interview where this issue arose, there was a favorable impression of the receptivity and helpfulness of both the staff and the board. Bruce Evans, Ellen Gruber, and Jim Luck were each recognized as having developed a reputation for offering help and encouragement to grant applicants. While most interviewees simply voiced a positive opinion on the demeanor of board members, one objected that board members were unduly influenced by pressure; another felt that the BMIF board was the least "political" of any he had ever dealt with.

7. *Grant beneficiaries.* Several people felt that too little funding went to minority causes. One individual said the issue of poverty did not get enough attention. However, the person who voiced this view went on to indicate that BMIF understood and responded well to the urban environment and was extremely receptive rather than distant and cold.

This comment is indicative of the interviews. All the negative impressions or reservations regarding the achievements of the foundation were overpowered by the positive appreciation of its accomplishments. The interviews were not designed to solicit either positive or negative responses. Rather, each began with, "You had expectations for the Battelle Foundation. How did it do?" The community leaders interviewed collectively answered that it did very well indeed.

Grant Recipient Reactions

The survey of recipients, a description of the survey's methodology, and a summary of the findings are carried in the appendixes. Findings and opinions of the recipients appear in the ensuing chapters. Some general observations and opinions of the recipients, however, are interesting, particularly when compared with views of the community leaders just cited.

Overall, the evaluation of the board, the foundation staff, and the process used to distribute funds was positive. There were almost no recommendations on how the funding process could have been changed, other than the observation by some that they would have preferred a more timely decision on their grants. Opinion was divided in grantee perceptions of the criteria and priorities followed by the BMIF board. While 68 percent of the respondents gave a positive response on that point, 32 percent reacted negatively. This would appear to suggest either opposition to the perceived priorities of the board, a lack of understanding of the board's priorities, or both.

Regarding the impact made by the BMIF grant on the agency itself, 79 percent of the 90 respondents indicated they had accomplished precisely the objectives outlined in their original grant proposal. Many of the cases discussed in the following chapters show that. An analysis of the questionnaire responses indicates an immediate impact on agencies in the areas of services performed, personnel employed, additional matching funds that were raised as a result of the BMIF grant, and expansion of physical facilities.

The opinions of the grantees reflected in the questionnaire were followed up by interviews with officials of agencies that had received grants. These interviews, many of which are referred to in the succeeding four chapters, suggest some general impressions of the impact of the BMIF grants upon their organizations. The evidence of impact most often heard was that the BMIF grant gave credibility to agency programs. Increased visibility was often cited by the officials of relatively new agencies. With older agencies, increased stability was often cited. Enhancement of the fund-raising capacity of the agencies receiving grants was also frequently mentioned. The timeliness of the grant was a common theme, particularly in the social agencies and arts organizations.

Reactions of Agencies Not Funded

R ecipients can hardly be expected to be negative about their grants or the foundation that made them. But what about those who requested grants, but did not receive them? The 700 grant requests that were declined were analyzed. A few grants, representative of proposals that had been given serious consideration, were selected for further analysis.

Interviews were conducted with seven representatives from a dozen such agenices.[4] As in earlier interviews conducted with community leaders, respondents were not given selected questions or propositions other than the general question, "From your experience with BMIF, what is your opinion of the foundation in its operation and the impact it has had on central Ohio?" All expressed themselves freely and succinctly. There were positive and negative responses to the foundation processes the applicants had experienced. One felt there had not been sufficient guidance from the foundation staff in writing a proposal to meet the guidelines. Another was very disappointed that, despite an invitation, no BMIF staff visit was made to the agency. Another repeated the disappointment about the lack of a site visit as well as some frustration about too abrupt a letter declining the grant request. One reported a BMIF board member relayed, "on the side," the specifics of the board's discussion and decision to decline the request. This left the respondent with a feeling of dissatisfaction rather than with the intended placation. Three others expressed satisfaction with BMIF procedures and behavior despite the lack of success of the proposal.

Several of those interviewed felt BMIF tended to fund strong, viable agencies and gave less attention to new or struggling ones. Several were cognizant of their own failure to develop a good proposal or to do so at the appropriate time. One emphasized that working on the BMIF proposal and experiencing the disappointment helped firm up the determination to move ahead anyway.

Finally, two of those interviewed expressed their satisfaction that the history of BMIF would allow the voice of an unsuccessful grant applicant to be heard.

The following chapters address the question of BMIF's impact on central Ohio by examining the objectives and consequences of the foundation's grants in specific areas. They include the arts and humanities, social services and health, education, and civic affairs. Each chapter is accompanied by a list of all grants in that particular area and charts displaying the dollar volume of activities supported and type of community benefit served by the grants.

NOTES AND SOURCES

Notes

1. An exhibit entitled "Characteristics of BMIF Grants" is carried in Appendix A. It contains an alphabetical listing of agencies, including a description of the project, year of grant, amount requested, and amount received, and codes the grant by type of institution, activity of the grant, and the aspect of community that benefited.

2. American Association of Fund-Raising Council, Inc., *Giving USA,* 26th Annual Issue (New York: 1981), p. 15.

3. Complete notes were taken of each interview. While not cited in the manuscript, all notes are available in the papers of the BMIF history project.

4. Interviews were by telephone. Notes are filed in the papers of the BMIF history project.

Sources

Interviews:

Sherwood L. Fawcett, president, Battelle Memorial Institute, Columbus, Ohio, November 4, 1980

Jack Gibbs, executive director, Ft. Hayes Career Center, Columbus, Ohio, November 14, 1980

Everett Reese, retired savings and loan association executive, Columbus, Ohio, November 20, 1980

William Guthrie, retired savings and loan association executive, Columbus, Ohio, November 21, 1980

Hon. Tom Moody, mayor, city of Columbus, Columbus, Ohio, November 24, 1980

Richard Trelease, executive director, Metropolitan Area Church Board, Columbus, Ohio, November 24, 1980

John Galbreath, owner, John W. Galbreath & Company, real estate subdividers and developers, Columbus, Ohio, November 25, 1980

Hon. Robert Duncan, judge, United States District Court, Columbus, Ohio, December 1, 1980

Amos Lynch, editor, *Call and Post,* Columbus, Ohio, December 3, 1980

Alfred Dietzel, president, Columbus Area Chamber of Commerce, Columbus, Ohio, December 3, 1980

Jerry Hammond, councilman, city of Columbus, Columbus, Ohio, December 5, 1980

Kline Roberts, lawyer and retired president, Columbus Area Chamber of Commerce, Columbus, Ohio, December 5, 1980

Mrs. Richard Witkind, citizen, Columbus, Ohio, January 21, 1981

Mary Lazarus, citizen, Columbus, Ohio, January 21, 1981

Leslie Bostic, executive director, Buckeye Boys Ranch, Columbus, Ohio, December 14, 1981

Joreece Smith, executive director, South Side Day Care Center, Columbus, Ohio, December 15, 1981

Billie Brown, executive director, Neighborhood House, Columbus, Ohio, December 16, 1981

Roger Germany, executive director, Hilltop Civic Council, Columbus, Ohio, December 16, 1981

Helen McDaniel, executive director, Catholic Social Service, Columbus, Ohio, December 16, 1981

Rev. Leon Troy, chairman of the board, Columbus Laboratory School, Columbus, Ohio, December 18, 1981

Robert Miller, director of development, Riverside Methodist Hospital, Columbus, Ohio, December 21, 1981

"

*As a result
of BMIF grants,
the arts
community
in Columbus
is richer, both
financially
and culturally,
more diversified,
stronger, and
more visible*

"

CHAPTER IV

The Arts and Humanities

At the time of BMIF's founding, the arts in Columbus were in a state of flux and growth. In the mid- to late-1960s, new sources of funding for the arts had been created—the most notable being the National Endowment for the Arts (NEA) and the Ohio Arts Council (OAC). Federal funding had expanded, and the economy was booming.

In 1969, there was a massive community effort to save the Ohio Theatre. With the assistance of a $750,000 matching gift from Battelle Memorial Institute and contributions from more than 3,500 individuals, companies, and foundations, the Columbus Association for the Performing Arts (CAPA) carried out the largest fund-raising campaign ever conducted for the performing arts in central Ohio. It prevented the demolition of the Ohio Theatre.

Several major building programs also began in the early 1970s, including one for the Columbus College of Art and Design and a new wing for the Columbus Gallery of Fine Arts. In 1971, Players Theatre, after years as a private club, opened its doors to the community. Art galleries were also being opened. A new director at the Columbus Gallery of Fine Arts replaced the director who had been with the gallery for 25 years before his retirement. After the demise of the Columbus Ballet, Ballet Metropolitan was founded. Dance, in general, was receiving new interest throughout the United States, and locally, Dancentral, Zivili, Ballet Metropolitan, and dance groups at area colleges and universities were responding to this increased interest.

In 1970, the Columbus Area Chamber of Commerce revived the Columbus Arts Council and, with a small, part-time staff, sponsored an annual arts festival on the statehouse lawn. Other programs sponsored by the council included an educational program called "Artists-in-Schools" and an arts calendar. In 1972-73, the Columbus Symphony Orchestra acquired its first full-time musicians, a string quartet and a woodwind quintet, and made plans to bring in more full-time musicians.

Cultural Explorations Study

Although a great deal of activity was occurring in the arts, there was so little coordination or communication that few people were aware of it. BMIF's Board of Trustees recognized early on that it needed guidance in evaluating how its money could be best distributed to the arts community. Early in the fall of 1975, G. C. Heffner and others met in Washington with Nancy Hanks, NEA executive director. Later in the year, several conferences and business luncheons were organized with outside art consultants and local arts, business, and civic leaders. It became apparent through these activities that there was a clear need to have a better picture of what cultural activities were taking place in Franklin County, who was doing what, and with what sources of funding.

While these activities were occurring at BMIF, the Junior League of Columbus was planning a small study on the arts as one of its regular task force projects. Heffner and others at BMIF heard about these plans and felt this was a possible solution to BMIF's need for a study. BMIF asked the league to expand its study to assess the current cultural activities in all of Franklin County. BMIF also asked for a determination of future needs of local arts groups and action plans necessary to meet those needs. The final product was expected to be a master plan for the arts in

Franklin County that would guide BMIF in evaluating requests from arts groups in the community.

BMIF Grants in the Arts and Humanities

AGENCY	AWARD
Columbus Symphony Orchestra	$1,000,000
Columbus Museum of Art	741,758
Columbus Association for the Performing Arts	500,000
Players Club Foundation	285,000
Columbus Association for the Performing Arts	251,000
Ballet Metropolitan	200,000
Columbus Museum of Art	100,000
Greater Columbus Arts Council	75,000
Kenyon College	75,000
Greater Columbus Arts Council	65,000
Dancentral	45,000
Greater Columbus Arts Council	35,000
American Council for the Arts in Education	25,000
Ballet Metropolitan	24,000
Ohio Program in Humanities	22,500
Greater Columbus Arts Council	17,500
Pro Musica Chamber Orchestra	15,000
Columbus Junior Theater of the Arts	10,000
Foundation of the Columbus Chapter of the American Institute of Architects	10,000
Hospital Audiences	10,000
Intermuseum Conservation Association	10,000
National Committee-Arts for the Handicapped	9,000
Zivili Kolo Ensemble	9,000
Zivili Kolo Ensemble	6,000

At the June 7, 1976, meeting, the BMIF Board of Trustees approved the proposal of the Junior League Arts Research Task Force for an assessment of the arts in Franklin County and authorized reimbursement to the league for "expenses incurred in connection with the study in an amount not to exceed $2,000." This was in addition to the $2,000 originally authorized for the study at the January 5, 1976, board meeting.

In September, the Junior League task force advised the board it could not accomplish an assessment of the arts in Columbus within the original financial arrangement. The following month, the league requested $36,200 to underwrite a professionally conducted assessment of cultural

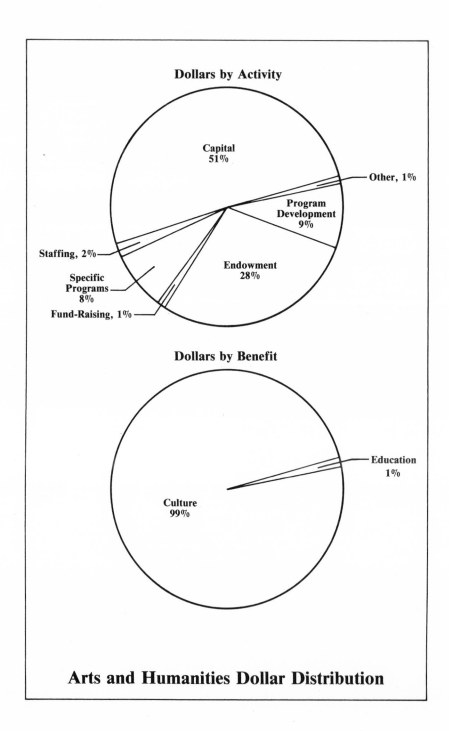

Dollars by Activity

Capital
51%

Other, 1%

Program
Development
9%

Staffing, 2%

Endowment
28%

Specific
Programs
8%

Fund-Raising, 1%

Dollars by Benefit

Education
1%

Culture
99%

Arts and Humanities Dollar Distribution

activities in Franklin County by an outside consulting company, Arts Development Associates, Inc., of Minneapolis and New York.

The board approved the following goals and objectives of the study on November 1, 1976:

1. Document the present cultural activities in Franklin County.

2. Determine who benefits from, and participates in, current arts activities, and the sources and levels of current financial support.

3. Determine future needs and goals for Franklin County's cultural development.

4. Develop action plans to meet future needs/goals and provide a community forum to consider initial findings.

This six-month arts assessment of Franklin County, called Cultural Explorations, was launched in December 1976. Originally, four areas of exploration were selected: artists and art organizations; current audiences for the arts; key leadership, including business, government, industry, labor, and funding sources; and community service and educational organizations.

The Cultural Explorations study was highlighted by a two-day conference in April 1977, attended by approximately 125 individuals who represented the four target areas previously studied. The conference was designed to develop a common vision of what the arts could be in Franklin County and how to reach that vision. One major assignment of the conference participants was to set priorities for the future. The following 11 items were suggested by the participants:

1. A strong, coordinative body for the arts.

2. Establishing a professional repertory theater.

3. A stronger symphony orchestra.

4. Reinstating and expanding the Arts Impact.

5. Developing an individual artists' service center.

6. Programs of audience development.

7. Expanding and improving the Artists-in-Schools program.

8. Strengthening the Gallery of Fine Arts.

9. Establishing a professional dance company.

10. Importing high-quality arts and professional artistic talents from outside the Columbus area.

11. Programs for the beautification of the urban environment.

The Cultural Explorations study generated considerable attention and interest in the arts. It also raised expectations and anticipation for the final report, distributed in June 1977. It is not surprising that many were disappointed in the final outcome. Each group had hoped that its needs and concerns would be the subject of major attention in the report.

The primary recommendation of the Cultural Explorations report, and the only one where any consensus was noted, was that the community establish a "strong coordinative body for the arts."

Greater Columbus Arts Council

The Cultural Explorations study made it clear that the community wanted and supported a larger role for the Greater Columbus Arts Council (GCAC). At the time, it was responsible only for running the annual arts festival, providing a monthly calendar of events, and distributing the city's support funds to the three major arts institutions.

For GCAC to assume new and broader responsibilities, certain changes were necessary. GCAC applied to BMIF in June 1977 for a grant of $223,000 over a three-year period to fund new programs and to hire a new, full-time experienced executive director and support staff.

BMIF responded by awarding GCAC a $65,000 two-year grant for salaries for an executive director and secretary. In the spring of 1978 following a nationwide search, Ric Wanetik, former associate director of the Cleveland Area Arts Council, was hired as GCAC's executive director. During Wanetik's first year, GCAC was restructured, and the trustees completed a long-range planning project that included an evaluation of the philosophy and procedures of the city of Columbus Grants Program for the Arts. GCAC increased its staff from four to seven full-time employees and restructured staff responsibilities. Other accomplishments included selecting Columbus as one of six cities for a study of the impact of arts organizations on local economies. GCAC also helped to influence Columbus City Council to pass a one percent tax on hotel rooms as an allotment for art in public places, and sponsored the second Business/Government/Arts Symposium attended by over 90 local leaders. Without question, GCAC was moving ahead with direction and visibility.

In June 1979, GCAC requested $125,000 from BMIF over a two-year period to help fund the implementation of a technical assistance program. BMIF awarded GCAC a total of $75,000 ($40,000 in 1979 and $35,000 in 1980) for this technical assistance program. GCAC used the grants to sponsor workshops and seminars on accounting, tax and book-keeping procedures, how to prepare slides to show off artist works, and how to pack and crate works of art. In addition, the council worked in cooperation with The Ohio State University College of the Arts to initiate Studies in Arts Management. These credit and noncredit courses are provided through the Continuing Education Division and College of the Arts. GCAC has also provided one-to-one consultation and guidance to individual artists and arts organizations who have technical problems or needs.

BMIF played a major role in this restructuring of GCAC. The impetus for change existed before BMIF entered the picture, but without the initial grant of $65,000 to fund the salary for an experienced, professional executive director, it is doubtful that this new direction would have occurred. Those closely affiliated with GCAC regard the BMIF grants as instrumental in remaking GCAC and helping it become the effective arts council it represents today.

Columbus Association for the Performing Arts

In March 1976, the Columbus Association for the Performing Arts (CAPA) requested $750,000 from BMIF to make major capital improvements to the Ohio Theatre. These included modernizing the heating and cooling systems, carpeting the entire theatre, updating the sound system, and remodeling the lighting, restrooms, and seating. The application pointed out that in the six years of CAPA's existence more than $823,900 had been spent for improvements to the theatre. CAPA argued that it would not be able to raise these funds in any one-year fund drive. The need to make these improvements was great, and the longer they were delayed the greater the final cost. In addition, the overall effect of the theatre's image and its ability to attract more patrons would be affected.

BMIF approved a grant of $500,000 to CAPA for these capital improvements. After receiving the money, CAPA gave priority to its three most crucial needs: improving the heating, ventilating, and air conditioning systems; replacing the 50-year-old carpet; and modernizing the sound system. In addition to the $500,000 from BMIF for these improvements, CAPA received two preservation grants from the U.S. Department of the Interior for $49,140, a $1,000 grant from the Harry C. Moores Foundation, and $83,532 from its own capital fund drive.

In February 1978, CAPA requested additional assistance, this time to expand the stage of the Ohio Theatre. It asked for $350,000 of the total $1.3 million needed to finish the job. Since the Ohio Theatre was originally built as a movie theater, it had only a small, shallow stage. In order to accommodate ballet, opera, and some theatrical productions, a much larger stage was needed. As a result of the Capitol Square South Development project, land was suddenly available behind the theatre to accomplish the expansion. Moreover, CAPA had received a three-to-one challenge grant from NEA. In order to take maximum advantage of that grant, CAPA needed to raise nearly $1.5 million in less than two years. The grant from BMIF would help make the stage expansion possible, and help CAPA maximize its NEA challenge grant to the fullest. At its March 6, 1978, meeting, the BMIF board approved a grant of $250,000 to expand the stage of the Ohio Theatre.

Having the Ohio Theatre available as a performing arts facility has greatly increased the number of cultural performances in Columbus. The theatre is currently the home of the Columbus Symphony Orchestra, Ballet Metropolitan, Jazz Arts Group, and Columbus Junior Theatre of the Arts. The BMI and BMIF affiliation with CAPA has served to provide funds for the purchase and restoration of the Ohio Theatre. Regardless of the confusion about CAPA's role in the community, one can clearly see the impact of the Battelle grants to the Ohio Theatre and CAPA in the improvements of the arts in Columbus.

Impact on Selected Art Institutions

The discussion up to this point has concentrated on the arts in a broad perspective and on institutions that have coordinated the arts and provided facilities for them. This section focuses on individual disciplines—dance, music, theater, and the visual arts—and how BMIF affected them.

DANCE. The largest grant to dance was a three-year $200,000 grant given to Ballet Metropolitan to allow the organization to become a professional ballet company in central Ohio. Ballet Metropolitan was founded in August 1974 after the Columbus Ballet failed because of financial problems. A group of concerned citizens, largely parents of children studying and dancing with the former company, decided to organize the new Ballet Metropolitan in order to retain its artistic director, Mrs. Tatjana Akinfieva-Smith, and its ballet mistress, Mrs. Daryl Kamer. They also wanted to continue to provide an opportunity for young ballet students to dance. The company was incorporated in September 1974 and gave its first performance of the *Nutcracker* that

Ballet Metropolitan's 1980 Nutcracker *season set new records for the company.*

December, selling almost 3,700 tickets and realizing a profit of $6,600. By 1977, the company was performing the *Nutcracker* with the Columbus Symphony Orchestra, and its four performances that year attracted over 9,000 people. Profits from the performances were $23,000.

In September 1976, Ballet Metropolitan appointed a planning committee to explore how the company could become professional. The planning committee's report, issued in June 1977, concluded that Ballet Metropolitan had the basic skills for training dancers and had the potential to evolve into a professional company. From this assessment came a five-year plan of growth and a decision to move ahead to become a resident professional ballet company in Columbus. The first priority was to obtain an artistic director and acquire permanent funding to broaden performance capacity and audience appeal. In July 1977, Ballet Metropolitan asked for and received a $33,000 grant from The Columbus Foundation to underwrite the salary and expenses of a director for a two-year period.

The next step toward the goal of becoming professional was the request for major funding from BMIF. Having followed a ballet company that had expired because of financial problems, Ballet Metropolitan operated conservatively and had prepared a solid five-year expansion program. In June 1978, BMIF's Board of Trustees approved a grant of $200,000, half the amount requested. The grant was to be distributed over a three-year period with $100,000 the first year, up to $60,000 the second year on a dollar-for-dollar match, and up to $40,000 in the third year on a one-for-two match. The effect of this reduced funding was that it decreased the number of professional dancers the company could hire in the first two years from 15 to 12 and forced the company to accelerate its fund-raising and audience development programs. Expanding the fund-raising drive turned out to be less difficult than expected, for "with the BMIF Stamp of Approval as perceived by the community, we were able to accomplish almost as much as we would have accomplished with full funding."[1]

In July 1978, Ballet Metropolitan became Columbus's first professional ballet company. During the first year of operation, the company performed before 32,900 persons and raised more than $75,955 to match the BMIF grant. In addition to the *Nutcracker* performances and a spring concert, Ballet Metropolitan participated in the Artists-in-Schools program, in the Dancebelt series, as well as in several small lectures and demonstrations. In 1979, the company performed before 61,946 persons, and its annual operating fund drive raised more than $44,000. The 1980-81 season saw the introduction of a fall concert along with a spring program and traditional *Nutcracker* performances. Ballet Metropolitan's 1980 *Nutcracker* set new records for the company. More than 23,500 persons saw the nine performances of this classic ballet, and the company grossed more than $175,000 and realized profits of nearly $75,000.

When it became professional in 1978, Ballet Metropolitan had a company of 12 professional dancers, an administrative staff of three full-time and two part-time individuals, and an operating budget of $290,000. In the 1980-81 season, it had 14 professional dancers, a staff of seven full-time and two part-time employees, and an operating budget of $550,000 that included the company's ballet school, Ballet Metropolitan Academy, acquired in August 1980. Excluding the school, the operating budget for 1980-81 was $482,000. In March 1981, BMIF awarded the company a grant of $24,000 to help subsidize its 1981-82 marketing and communication programs intended to generate additional income. In 1980-81, the company earned 60 percent of its income, compared with the national average of 55 percent, and set a goal to achieve 65 percent by the end of 1982.

Ballet was not the only form of dance that BMIF supported. It also gave assistance to a professional modern dance company. Dancentral was an outgrowth of a professional modern dance company, American Dance in Repertory, founded at Ohio State in 1969. Ruth Currier, the company's director, left Ohio State in 1972 to become artistic director of the Jose Limon Company in New York City, and the university company folded. In 1973, Maggie Patton, who had been a soloist and choreographer for American Dance in Repertory and had taught dance at the university for over ten years, formed her own company, Dancentral. Dancentral began with a small group of highly qualified dancers/teachers/choreographers without any financial backing. In 1977, Dancentral decided to expand and become Columbus's only professional modern dance company.

In February 1978, Dancentral applied to BMIF for a $111,705 grant over a three-year period to help provide the foundation for a professional company. This funding would allow Dancentral to pay its dancers the AGMA (American Guild of Musical Artists) minimum wage for the first time, as well as commission new choreography, increase promotional activities, and add a company business manager and apprentice director. In its March 1978 meeting, the BMIF board awarded Dancentral $45,000 over a three-year period, representing $15,000 per year for dancer salaries.

Although BMIF's grant was less than half the amount Dancentral requested, it allowed the company to pay its dancers and to continue its dance concert series. More important, the Battelle grant gave the company credibility and visibility within the community. According to Maggie Patton, corporate fund-raising became possible for the first time. Dancentral was no longer an unsure, untried organization. In retrospect, Patton concluded, receiving less than the requested amount was probably advantageous to the development of the company. It was more feasible to move gradually to a budget of more than $100,000 and be able to sustain it with community support.

Dancentral has grown dramatically since the late 1970s. Its total operating budget in 1976 was $8,500, while its approved budget for 1981 was $70,100. The budget included salaries for five contract dancers on an 18-week schedule and an artistic director, a part-time secretary, and a part-time business director and manager. By 1985, Dancentral hopes to have a 50-week rehearsal and performance schedule, a 15-week touring season, eight salaried professional dancers, an artistic director, a general manager, a development/public relations director, and an education director. Its future, like many performing arts groups, remains somewhat uncertain because of the constant need to raise money. Bookings and teaching provide only about 50 percent of its annual budget. But the company's goal is to be a nationally recognized contemporary dance company.

Zivili Kolo Ensemble began in 1973 when three women of Croatian descent met in Columbus and created a dance company. Zivili started with 12 dancers, singers, and musicians and performed at picnics, fairs, and other special events. By 1977, the number of dancers in the company had increased to 30, and the group had performed throughout Ohio and in Florida. In November 1977, Zivili requested $12,000 from BMIF to provide funds to help support three staff positions: artistic director, music director, and business manager. At its December 5, 1977, meeting, BMIF's board awarded Zivili $9,000.

The BMIF grant gave Zivili important visibility throughout the community. The grant came early in the company's existence and helped Zivili develop and grow professionally. In 1978, Zivili received a $15,000 grant from the Ohio Arts Council that allowed the company to pay its dancers $100 per month for a five-month season. It was the first time the dancers had received any salary. In early 1979, Zivili asked BMIF for $180,000 over a three-year period to continue to provide salaries for its 30 performers. BMIF denied the request. What apparently had not been made clear in the proposal was how Zivili intended to fund its dancers after the three-year grant expired. In retrospect, even those closely associated with Zivili feel that the organization benefited by growing stronger more gradually than would have been possible if it had received the $180,000 grant.

In February 1981, Zivili applied to BMIF for a $6,000 grant to help it equip and move into new headquarters at the Croatian Hall in Columbus. The board approved the request in March 1981. The new headquarters not only gave Zivili a place to display Yugoslavian artifacts and its ethnic research collection, but also allowed it to offer dance classes for the first time.

The role BMIF played in the dance movement of Columbus was significant. It is too soon to say how well all the dance companies will fare in the next ten to 15 years, but they are obviously financially and artistically stronger today because of the assistance BMIF provided.

THEATER. Throughout the Cultural Explorations study, strong interest was expressed in a professional repertory theater. In the list of priorities for the arts in Columbus, establishment of a professional theater was second only to the need for a coordinating body for the arts.

Columbus has many community theaters; the best known is the Players Theatre. Founded in 1923 as a private club, but open to the entire community since 1974, the Players Theatre is the oldest community-oriented theatre in Ohio and one of the oldest in the nation. In August 1976, the theatre applied to BMIF for $25,500 to replace its heating plant and to install air conditioning so it could operate year-round rather than just during its nine-month season. The extended season would have resulted in three additional major productions per year and increased revenues and patrons. At its September 1976 meeting, the BMIF board turned down the request largely because the capital improvements for which the grant had been requested had been completed and financial arrangements had already been made to pay for them. The BMIF grant would have merely offset a planned deficit.

In August 1978, Players Theatre returned to BMIF requesting $535,000 for major expansion and renovation of its facilities on Franklin Avenue. Although there had been discussions about relocating the theatre, the Players board wanted to maintain its downtown location for centrality and for historical reasons. However, major improvements would be necessary. The roof leaked, the wiring was a fire hazard, and the theatre was too small. While these plans were being made, adjacent property that would provide space for expansion became available and Players Theatre bought it. At its September 1978 meeting, the BMIF board approved a grant of $285,000, $35,000 as an outright gift and a $250,000 dollar-for-dollar matching grant. In less than a year, in the largest capital fund drive in its history, Players Theatre raised enough funds to receive the full BMIF grant.

Players Theatre opened its newly renovated
and expanded theatre complex on October 17, 1980.

On October 17, 1980, Players Theatre opened its newly renovated and expanded complex. The theatre now accommodates 1,560 patrons in the main stage Shedd Theatre and 350 in the intimate Van Fleet Theatre. It was able to add new space for a lobby, scene shop, costume room, prop room, dressing rooms, and offices. Since becoming a community organization, Players Theatre has grown from an annual budget of $40,000 in 1973 with an executive director and a part-time secretary to a 1980 budget of $265,000 and 11 full-time staff members. In addition, the audience has increased dramatically, from 9,740 in 1973 to over 17,570 in the 1979-80 season.

BMIF assisted another developing repertory group, The Kenyon Festival Theater in Gambier, Ohio. In May 1980, BMIF awarded $75,000 to the theater to assist in developing a high-quality professional company. In its first year of operation, the theater raised $225,000 in additional funds. In accord with its original plan, the group presented a series of plays during a three-month summer festival on the Kenyon College campus and took up residence in Columbus in the winter of 1983.

M USIC. BMIF's largest contribution to the arts was a $1 million grant to the Columbus Symphony Orchestra to endow five new full-time positions and to expand the symphony's educational services.

The Cultural Explorations study uncovered feelings of dissatisfaction with the symphony and a strong desire among many that Columbus should have a major symphony orchestra. A strengthened symphony orchestra was the third most important priority selected by the final conference of the Cultural Explorations study. After the study was completed, the Columbus Symphony Orchestra submitted a proposal to BMIF requesting $1.2 million to add five full-time musicians and to expand its educational services. At its March 1978 meeting, the BMIF board approved a grant of $1 million, $800,000 to endow five chairs and $200,000 for program development.

Until 1972, all members of the Columbus Symphony Orchestra had been part-time. The first full-time musicians to be hired constituted a string quartet, followed by a woodwind quintet in the 1973-74 season. In 1978-79, the symphony added another string quartet and bass player and used the BMIF grant to hire a third string quartet, bringing the total number of full-time musicians to 18. The symphony's goal is to have a core of 40 full-time players by 1985. The addition of full-time professional musicians increases not only the quality of the symphony, but also

*The Columbus Symphony Woodwind Quintet plays
before an appreciative audience of school children.*

*The beautiful "Walled Garden" at the
Columbus Museum of Art.*

the personnel available to perform services in the community, such as more Artists-in-Schools programs, music in the parks, and other small lecture and demonstration events.

In its 30-year history, the Columbus Symphony Orchestra has grown from a three-concert series with all-volunteer musicians to a season that includes four different subscription series—pop, symphonic, opera, and chamber. It now has 18 full-time musicians among its more than 80 members. The budget has grown from $12,263 in 1951-52 to $1.7 million in 1980-81.

The Cultural Explorations report that recommended Columbus have a major symphony orchestra has not yet been fully realized, but the BMIF grant gave that goal a boost and challenged the community to join in bringing it to reality.

VISUAL ARTS. In September 1977, BMIF gave the Columbus Museum of Art $741,758, the largest single-source grant in the museum's history. The grant was to be used to renovate one wing of the museum, to consolidate and increase exhibition space, to increase space for public amenities, to add a public restaurant, and to consolidate the staff work area. More dramatically, the grant provided for the creation of a major sculpture garden.

In order to improve the display area and to make the museum more inviting and efficient, Budd Bishop, director of the museum, wanted to make some major renovations, particularly to the new wing. In addition, Bishop felt the outside facade of the museum was formidable and not inviting to the public. Having had previous experience with a small sculpture garden at a museum in Chattanooga, Tennessee, Bishop wanted to explore that possibility in Columbus. He believed that a well-designed sculpture garden and several important pieces of sculpture would make the Columbus museum different from others in Ohio and would provide an inviting atmosphere to attract new audiences.

In the spring and summer of 1977, the museum prepared its proposal to renovate and develop the sculpture garden. Work began immediately after BMIF's approval of the museum's full request of $741,758. Meanwhile, the museum continued its annual fund drives so it could eliminate its deficit and accumulate a cash surplus to avoid borrowing. In November 1976, the museum established its first Department of Development to organize all fund-raising, membership, and public relations activities. The first annual operating fund drive was held in early 1977 with a goal of $554,275. The campaign reached 98 percent of its goal, raising $540,127, a 220 percent increase over 1976 contributions.

In addition, the museum received a challenge grant of $260,000 from the National Endowment for the Humanities in early 1977 that required a three-to-one match within three years. This grant gave a new impetus to the fund drive. In its second annual drive in 1978, the museum achieved 94 percent of its announced goal or $545,000, and in 1979, it reached 93 percent of its goal or $580,000. In addition, city, county, and state support also increased during 1979, such that nearly nine percent of the museum's annual operating budget was supported by government agencies.

The growth of the museum can be seen in the expansion of its annual budget as well as its increased fund-raising goals. In 1976, the museum had an operating budget of $720,000, of which $100,000 was a budgeted deficit. In 1980, the museum's operating budget was $1.3 million, with over $400,000 in cash reserves. Membership also increased, although not as dramatically as the director and staff would have liked.

The Columbus Museum of Art illustrates, in a most dramatic manner, how grants given at the critical time in the history of an organization can have a mushrooming effect far greater than the grant itself. The museum obtained an enthusiastic new director who, through BMIF, had a large sum of money available to enact plans in a dramatic way. This achievement not only strengthened the hand of the new director, but also improved the fund-raising capability of the museum. Once again, BMIF money was a catalyst in the community, encouraging other individuals and corporations to give. Since the museum did not have to use its annual fund drive receipts to pay for needed improvements, it was able to attract more givers, eliminate its debt, and create a surplus much faster than would have been otherwise possible.

In June 1979, the sculpture garden was opened to the public, with several magnificent pieces of donated sculpture on display. In September 1980, the Museum of Modern Art in New York loaned the Columbus museum six large sculptures. The sculpture garden has not only made a dramatic visual change in the appearance of the museum, but has also made it more appealing and attractive to passersby. In addition, the uniqueness of the sculpture garden draws people from other cities in Ohio and from other states. BMIF's second gift to the museum came in July 1981, with an award of $100,000 to help fund the acquisition of a major work of sculpture to replace the works on loan from the Musuem of Modern Art.

Artists-in-Schools Program

The Artists-in-Schools program began in 1970 when NEA made funds available to five school systems across the country to determine the impact of arts on children's attitudes toward learning and behavior problems. When the funding ended, the Columbus Public Schools and OAC provided additional funds for one year, but the costs were too high to allow the program to continue.

GCAC's proposal to BMIF requested $52,500 for program and administrative costs for one year of operation of the Artists-in-Schools program for 15 Columbus public schools and 15 suburban, private, parochial, and county elementary schools. In December 1975, BMIF approved a grant of $17,500, providing the rest could be raised from other sources. With this grant, the Artists-in-Schools program was able to secure another $17,500 grant from The Columbus Foundation. In addition, the Junior League and OAC also contributed funds, allowing the program to be continued and expanded in 1976-77.

In June 1977, GCAC asked BMIF for an additional $35,000 to continue and expand the Artists-in-Schools program over a two-year period. The success of the program had been clearly evident in the evaluations and response from the community and from other foundation support for the program. The BMIF board approved the request in the full amount of $17,500 for school year 1977-78 and $17,500 for school year 1978-79, with the understanding that the Artists-in-Schools program would seek new sources of funding thereafter and would not be dependent on continued funding from BMIF.

The impact of the Artists-in-Schools program on the community has exceeded the original expectations. As part of their regular schooling, young children are exposed to the enrichment and excitement of encounters with professional artists in drama, dance, music, visual arts, and photography. The program also creates a new audience for the arts and provides financial support and exposure for local artists.

In 1980-81, the Artists-in-Schools program was part of GCAC's Assistance Program and received its major funding from the portion of the hotel/motel city tax earmarked for GCAC. The Artists-in-Schools program provides services and consultation to area artists and arts organizations and serves as a link between elementary and middle schools and the city's professional arts resources. In 1979, over 50,000 children saw 900 in-school performances, lectures, or workshops.

One critical aspect of increasing support for the arts is building the arts audience; the best way to accomplish that goal is to reach out and involve young people at the critical stages of their lives, to make the arts a natural part of their lives, and thereby raise the aesthetic sensibility of the community. In essence, this is what the Artists-in-Schools program seeks to accomplish.

Conclusion

Within a period of five and one-half years, BMIF gave more than $3.5 million to the arts community in Columbus and central Ohio. How has this money changed the arts in Columbus, and what will be the impact when this source of funding ends? The earlier sections have shown that BMIF grants, in many cases, made a dramatic impact on individual organizations as well as on the community. Some organizations such as Ballet Metropolitan, GCAC, and Kenyon Festival Theater might not exist in their present form without the BMIF grants. Others, such as the museum and the symphony, have been significantly strengthened and made more visible in the community as a result of the funding.

Several significant trends appear throughout all the arts organizations that received BMIF grants. These include the development or evolution of professionalism within the organizations, the impact of the Battelle name in establishing validity and credibility within the community, and the importance of timing of the grant within the particular development of the organization.

Several organizations in Columbus were at a critical stage of development in the early 1970s. The BMIF grants made it possible for many to solidify or create professional positions that otherwise might have taken many years to establish. The museum was taking on new life with a new director whose first act was to hire a professional development officer and to begin analyzing the personnel needs and procedures of the museum. The symphony also was moving toward more professionalism, although at a somewhat slower pace. In 1978-79, the symphony hired its first director of public relations and created its first professional development office in 1979-80. GCAC had first been staffed with volunteers as part of the Columbus Area Chamber of Commerce, although its first director, Vonnie Sanford, was a paid employee. With the BMIF money, GCAC was able to hire its first professional executive director who sought other professionals to staff the organization. The BMIF grant to help establish a professional ballet company in Columbus allowed Ballet Metropolitan to hire a professional staff that included an artistic director, a general manager, and a director of development and public relations. In 1973, Players Theatre had only an executive director and a part-time secretary. The organization now has 11 full-time staff members including an executive director, a public relations director, a director of educational programming, and an audience development director.

The ability to complete this transition from voluntarism to professionalism in a shorter span of time removed some of the tensions that otherwise would have plagued some arts organizations. The danger, of course, is that *if* the organizations themselves are not able to maintain the financial level necessary to keep a professional staff, all will have suffered. It is quite clear, however, that BMIF made a concerted effort not to dampen the charitable generosity of the community and not to fund operating expenses or fund groups that seemed unlikely to succeed. The primary method of encouraging the community to donate more funds to the arts community was the matching grant concept. The process encouraged the organization to work harder to raise funds from the community.

These organizations often found it easier to raise money from the community with a BMIF grant. Several organization directors indicated that the Battelle name opened doors within the corporate community. The Battelle name also gave credibility to many smaller, less established organizations. For those who were established, a BMIF grant gave evidence of approval and support of their programs and direction. This "stamp of approval" that the Battelle name provided opened the doors not only within the Columbus area, but also within state and national organizations such as NEA and OAC. Thus, the BMIF grants for many organizations began a cycle of support that would not have been otherwise possible.

As a result of BMIF grants, the arts community in Columbus is richer, both financially and culturally, more diversified, stronger, and more visible.

NOTES AND SOURCES
Note
1. A Survey of Battelle Memorial Institute Foundation Grant Recipients. Impact: The Battelle Foundation, 1975-1981—Ballet Metropolitan, 1980.

Sources
Arts Development Associates, Inc., *Cultural Explorations for the Future in Franklin County,* a public planning project of the Junior League of Columbus, Ohio, June 1977.

Herb Cook, "Looking for Culture," *Columbus Monthly,* June 1977, pp. 59-66.

Johns Hopkins University, Center for Metropolitan Planning and Research, *The Economic Impact of Six Cultural Institutions on the Economy of the Columbus SMSA* (Baltimore, Maryland: Johns Hopkins University, Center for Metropolitan Planning and Research), December 1979.

Women's Association of the Columbus Symphony Orchestra, Inc., "A History of the First Fifteen Years of the Columbus Symphony Orchestra, 1951-1966," Columbus, Ohio, 1966.

Columbus Association for the Performing Arts, *The Ohio Theatre 1928-1978,* Columbus, Ohio, 1978.

Columbus Association for the Performing Arts, "The Report of the Cultural Explorations Committee on the Coordinative Body for the Arts," Columbus, Ohio, September 1977.

BMIF Files:

Battelle Memorial Institute Foundation case files of all arts and humanities organizations that submitted grant proposals, 1975-81.

A Survey of Battelle Memorial Institute Foundation Grant Recipients. Impact: The Battelle Foundation, 1975-1981—all arts recipients that returned questionnaire.

Interviews:

Maggie Patton, artistic director, Dancentral, Columbus, Ohio, September 15, 1980

Ed Graczyk, executive director, Players Theatre of Columbus, Columbus, Ohio, September 17, 1980

John Henle, chairman, Ohio Arts Council, Columbus, Ohio, September 19, 1980

Harvey Roth, managing director, Ballet Metropolitan, Columbus, Ohio, September 21, 1980

Herb Cook, associate publisher, *Columbus Monthly,* Columbus, Ohio, September 22, 1980

Melissa Obenauf, manager, Zivili: Songs and Dances of Yugoslavia, Columbus, Ohio, September 23, 1980

Budd Bishop, director, Columbus Museum of Art, Columbus, Ohio, September 26, 1980

James Buchanan, director of development, Columbus Museum of Art, Columbus, Ohio, September 26, 1980

Andrew Broekema, dean, College of the Arts, The Ohio State University, Columbus, Ohio, October 1, 1980.

Darrell Edwards, general manager, Columbus Symphony Orchestra, Columbus, Ohio, October 6, 1980

Susan Rosenstock, assistant manager, Columbus Symphony Orchestra, Columbus, Ohio, October 6, 1980

W. Bruce Evans, vice president for development, Franklin University, and former executive director, Battelle Memorial Institute Foundation, Columbus, Ohio, October 8, 1980

S. N. Hallock, executive director, Center of Science and Industry, Columbus, Ohio, October 8, 1980

Robert Karlsberger, Karlsberger and Associates, Architects, Inc., Columbus, Ohio, October 10, 1980

Mary Bishop, chairman of the Building Committee, Columbus Association for the Performing Arts, Columbus, Ohio, October 15, 1980

Mrs. Charles (Frances) Lazarus, vice president, Board of Trustees, Greater Columbus Arts Council, Columbus, Ohio, November 10, 1980

Mrs. James (Marilyn) Scanlan, member, Board of Trustees, Columbus Museum of Art, Columbus, Ohio, September 9, 1980

Mrs. Howard (Babs) Sirak, member, Board of Trustees, Columbus Museum of Art, Columbus, Ohio, October 27, 1980

Mrs. Edgar A. (Nancy) Strause, president, Board of Trustees, Ballet Metropolitan and former chairperson, Artists and Arts Organizations, Junior League's study on *Cultural Explorations for the Future in Franklin County,* Columbus, Ohio, September 22, 1980

Tim Sublette, assistant director, Greater Columbus Arts Council, Columbus, Ohio, September 8, 1980

Ric Wanetik, executive director, Greater Columbus Arts Council, Columbus, Ohio, September 8, 1980

Mrs. Richard (Shelie) Wolfe, member, Board of Trustees, Dancentral, Columbus, Ohio, October 1, 1980

"
*Most of the
social service
and
health agencies
funded by
BMIF
were well
established in
the community*
"

CHAPTER V

Social Services and Health

The federal government's war on poverty in the 1960s created a growing public awareness and heightened government concern for the social service and health needs of citizens. In the last two decades, there has been a dramatic increase in the public perception of human service needs, and programs and agencies to meet those needs have proliferated. Rapid growth also has taken place in programs and funding for health services, due primarily to the establishment of Medicare and Medicaid in 1965.

In the mid-1970s, federal funding policies changed, permitting more local decision-making in the allocation of funds, including those for social services and health programs. Since 1974, the city of Columbus has been responsible for distributing Federal Revenue Sharing funds and Title VI Comprehensive Employment and Training Act (CETA) funds. The Welfare Department allocates Title XX funds. During this period, the Columbus metropolitan area experienced rapid population growth, and social service needs increased and changed. The social service system grew into a vast and complex network of 300 to 400 separate private and public agencies. For the most part, each operated autonomously, and there was little communication and coordination between agencies.

City and county officials were confronted with the responsibility of allocating millions of dollars to the social services system without adequate information or criteria on which to base their decisions. This concern led Fran Ryan, a member of the Columbus City Council in 1975, to introduce a resolution citing the need for joint planning and coordination of the delivery of social services. This resolution was the impetus for the formation of a study committee, commonly referred to as the Lazarus Committee. The committee was named for its chairman, Charles Y. Lazarus, then chief executive officer of F. & R. Lazarus Company, the area's largest retail operation and one of the largest employers in Columbus.

The committee recommended the formation of a citizens' committee to investigate the social service system. The objective of the citizens' committee would be to develop a new model for the delivery of social services. The Citizens' Committee for Human Services was established in 1975 and included influential community, business, and civic leaders.

BMIF had an initial impact on the social service system by granting $200,000 to United Way to finance the Citizens' Committee for Human Services study. The grant allowed the committee to conduct a more comprehensive study than might otherwise have been possible. As a result of this study, the Metropolitan Human Services Commission (MHSC) was formed in 1976 as an information provider, coordinator, and planning resource for the social service system. MHSC's inventory of social services, its needs assessment survey, and a priority listing of social service programs completed in 1977 provided the data necessary for more informed decision-making in allocating social service funds. Dorothy Reynolds, then MHSC's vice president for program development, stated that the commission's most important achievement has been its contribution to the more informed decisions now being made in the social services area.

During the first three years of BMIF's existence, expenditures for social services in Franklin County from all government sources and United Way increased rapidly. MHSC reports that funding rose from $60 million in 1975 to more than $100 million in 1978. In 1977, over 200 agencies offered programs with nearly $100 million in funding available from approximately 100 sources of public and private funding. During the period in which BMIF operated, the public sector provided about 76 percent of the dollars expended by human service programs and the pri-

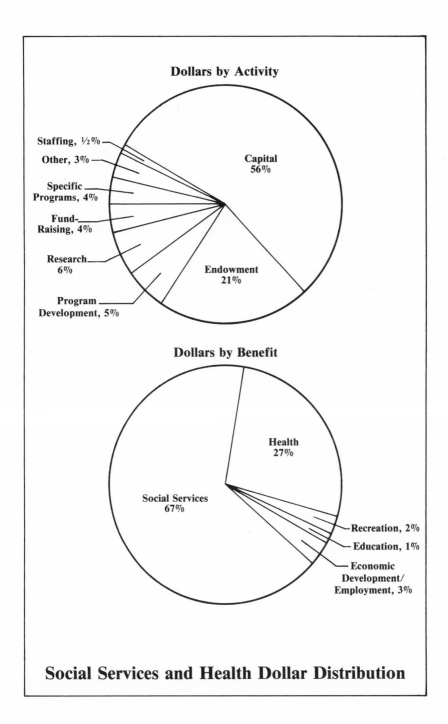

Dollars by Activity

Staffing, ½%

Other, 3%

Specific Programs, 4%

Fund-Raising, 4%

Research 6%

Program Development, 5%

Capital 56%

Endowment 21%

Dollars by Benefit

Social Services 67%

Health 27%

Recreation, 2%

Education, 1%

Economic Development/ Employment, 3%

Social Services and Health Dollar Distribution

vate sector provided 24 percent. Of those dollars provided by the private sector, foundations accounted for about seven percent and United Way provided another seven percent.[1]

Most of the social service and health agencies funded by BMIF were well established in the community. Several were affiliates of national organizations. Approximately one-third were United Way members.

BMIF Grants in Social Services and Health

AGENCY	AWARD
Children's Hospital Research Foundation	$1,501,743
United Way of Franklin County	1,000,000
Jewish Center of Columbus	500,000
YMCA of Columbus	480,000
Ohio School for the Deaf Alumni Association	321,000
Isabelle Ridgway Home for the Aged	300,000
Heinzerling Memorial Foundation	275,000
Columbus Urban League	250,000
United Way of Franklin County	200,000
YWCA of Columbus	200,000
Creative Living	162,500
Boy Scouts of America, Central Ohio Council	150,000
Goodwill Industries of Central Ohio	150,000
Hannah Neil Center for Children	150,000
South Side Settlement House	150,000
Mid-Ohio Health Planning Federation	125,000
Children's Hospital Research Foundation	106,833
American Red Cross	100,000
Planned Parenthood of Central Ohio	100,000
St. Stephen's Community House	100,000
United Way of Franklin County	100,000
YMCA of Licking County-Newark	100,000
North Area Mental Health and Retardation Services	98,337
Goodwill Industries of Central Ohio	86,000
Pilot Dogs	80,000
Harding Hospital	75,000
Southwest Community Mental Health Center	75,000
Delaware Speech and Hearing Center	56,000
Boy Scouts of America, Central Ohio Council	50,000
Columbus Area Council on Alcoholism	50,000
ECCO Family Health Center	50,000
Godman Guild Association	50,000
Goodwill Industries of Central Ohio	50,000
Metropolitan Women's Center	50,000

Seal of Ohio Girl Scout Council	50,000
Vision Center of Central Ohio	43,000
New Wineskins Center for Research and Development	42,000
Childhood League	40,000
Huckleberry House	40,000
Vision Center of Central Ohio	39,160
Epilepsy Association of Ohio	37,500
Ohio Developmental Disabilities	37,500
Boy Scouts of America, Central Ohio Council	35,000
Mental Health Association of Ohio	30,405
Choices for Victims of Domestic Violence	30,000
Liberty Community Center	30,000
St. Vincent Children's Center	30,000
The Salvation Army	30,000
Licking-Knox Goodwill Industries	27,427
Camp Fire Girls	25,000
Columbus Literacy Council	25,000
Junior Achievement	25,000
Starr Commonwealth for Boys	25,000
United Way of Franklin County	25,000
Grant Hospital	21,000
Family Counseling and Crittenton Services	20,000
Franklin County Halfway House	20,000
Phoenix House	20,000
Legal Aid Society of Columbus	18,000
Crippled Children's Center	16,000
Volunteer Action Center	15,250
Boys Clubs of Columbus	15,000
Central Ohio Heart Chapter	15,000
Senior Citizens Placement Bureau	15,000
Salesian Boys Club of Columbus	14,000
Legal Aid Society of Columbus	13,750
Columbus Speech and Hearing Center	12,000
Operation Feed	12,000
Central Ohio Radio Reading Service	11,000
Central Ohio Radio Reading Service	10,000
Community Coordinated Child Care	10,000
Legal Aid Society of Columbus	10,000
The Lighthouse	10,000
Senior Citizens Placement Bureau	10,000
Syntaxis	10,000
Columbus Speech and Hearing Center	7,000
Columbus Literacy Council	6,250
Starr Laneview Center	6,000
League Against Child Abuse	5,000
Franklin County Halfway House	2,600

Nearly all had broad community support and had demonstrated the ability to secure public and private funding. Most organization officials stated their agencies were able to continue serving community needs after BMIF funds had been distributed. The current cuts in social service funding may change this assessment for some agencies, especially for those relying primarily on federal funds. Some BMIF grants were awarded to financially troubled organizations that were providing services that the community recognized should be continued.

The greatest impact of BMIF grants for social service and health organizations was in helping to improve facilities. There is no comprehensive study available on the capital needs of social service and health organizations. Community leaders and social services personnel were asked whether capital improvement grants were the most appropriate distribution of BMIF funding in this area. They unanimously agreed that a tremendous capital improvement need existed, and that these improvements made the best use of BMIF funds. According to these organizations, raising money for program and operating expenses was easier than raising capital funds. Capital grants also affect programs and services by allowing organizations to provide new or expanded programs, serve more clients, hire additional staff, and improve the quality of the organization's service. In order to evaluate BMIF's impact in the areas of health and social services, the grants have been grouped into six functional categories: community-wide, neighborhood, children and teenagers, handicapped and developmentally disabled, senior citizens and women, and health and medical services. Several grants in each category will be examined to determine what impact the awards had on particular agencies. In addition, the general impact in the six areas will be assessed.

Community-wide Grants

Community-wide grants accounted for slightly over one-third of all grants in the social service category. About two-thirds of the grants in this area were for capital improvements. One agency, United Way of Franklin County, received nearly half the total capital expenditures for community-wide grants. Eight of the 11 grants went to organizations for research and program development, but the dollar expenditures were relatively small compared to the capital awards.

United Way received $200,000 to conduct the Citizens' Committee for Human Services study that led to the establishment of MHSC. It also received a grant of $1 million in 1978 to purchase its own building,

$100,000 for its supplementary campaign in 1980, and $25,000 in 1981. The United Way proposal to BMIF offered the following justifications for the purchase of a building: provision of low-rent office space for private and not-for-profit social service agencies; centralization of social service planning agencies within one building for better coordination and integration of social services; and provision of space for community social service meetings and proximity to the downtown business community. United Way's Battelle Human Services Building provides a downtown location and space for social service interaction. MHSC's offices are located in the building, but United Way has not yet attracted as many of the other social service agencies as was anticipated. United Way personnel believe, however, that a downtown location has increased its status, an important consideration for an organization that raises private funds for approximately 60 social service agencies.

The Jewish Center of Columbus received $500,000 in 1977 from BMIF to construct a new Community Life Center that would provide services for all age groups and a variety of programs including an expanded day care center, an auditorium for Columbus's only community orchestra, and intergenerational programs for youth, adults, and senior citizens. The building program was delayed due to a controversy over the site. The dispute has been resolved, and construction of the center began in 1981. Barton Schacter, former director of the center, described BMIF's gift as the catalyst that helped convince other foundations and private individuals to contribute to the project.

A $250,000 grant from BMIF also helped to establish the Center for Change and Leadership, a research arm of the Columbus Urban League. Frank Lomax, president of the league, cited the center's study and publication of the *State of Black Columbus* as an example of how research has elevated the status of the Urban League in the community. The research center completed a thorough study of Urban League clients and participated in a needs assessment study called *Black Pulse* that interviewed 3,000 black households in the nation. The data produced by the center gave credibility to the Urban League's voice in the community.

The Urban League grant was not restricted. BMIF trustees, however, preferred that the money be used as an endowment for the center. Lomax defended the league's decision to expend the funds over a period of three years on the grounds that the impact was greater than if smaller dollar expenditures had been spread over a longer period of time. In 1981, the survival of the Center for Change and Leadership as a separate Urban League affiliate was uncertain. However, Lomax said he believes that because of the experience and the success of the center, funding for further research will be built into Urban League programs.[2]

*The May 15, 1981, groundbreaking ceremony at the
Columbus Jewish Center for its new Community Life Center.*

A relatively modest grant can have a substantial impact on a small agency. One example is the Volunteer Action Center (VAC), which received $15,250 from BMIF. Established in 1970, the center is a clearinghouse for volunteers and volunteer administrators. The decreasing number of volunteers in the 1970s, paralleled by an increased awareness of the value of volunteer services, led VAC to apply for BMIF funding to conduct a survey of volunteers and nonvolunteers. The study's identification of the active, inactive, and potential volunteer was of special importance to social service agencies in an era of decreasing funds for paid staff. Glenn Esh, executive director of VAC, reported that the center coordinated several follow-up conferences and workshops for social service agencies. As a result of these sessions, two new networks have been established: the Volunteer Administrators Network and the Recruiting Employee Volunteers network, which helps secure volunteers from the Columbus business community. This represents a new direction for the agency and is based on the study's findings.

Alvis House, the Franklin County halfway house for ex-offenders, received two grants from BMIF, one for $2,600 to assist the organization in receiving accreditation from the National Commission on Accreditations for Corrections. Alvis House is one of only 20 accredited private halfway houses in the United States and Canada. A second $20,000 grant in 1980 provided start-up funds for a new program, a residential center for offenders diagnosed as mentally retarded. In this, as in other cases, BMIF's startup award had a significant impact since the funds were used to help secure additional funding. The grant helped document a need to be met within an already established agency.

Neighborhood Impact Grants

BMIF social service grants had a positive effect on organizations serving neighborhoods and communities in the central Ohio area. Eight well-established organizations received slightly over 20 percent of the total social service grants. All but one of these grants were for capital improvements. Both the Young Men's Christian Association (YMCA) of Columbus and the YMCA of Licking County, Newark, received awards for capital campaigns. Each YMCA now has a building that serves the entire family, provides new programs, and serves as a facility for use by other community organizations. The funds to the Columbus YMCA were used primarily to finish a branch facility that serves the northern area of Franklin County. In its first year of operation, the North Area YMCA served 12,000 new members. The Young Women's Christian

Association (YWCA) in downtown Columbus received a $200,000 grant that was used primarily for fire and safety code updates throughout the entire building. Nancy Shilling, director of the YWCA, anticipated that the BMIF grant will prove crucial in generating additional funds from the community in the forthcoming capital campaign.

Three neighborhood community centers—the South Side Settlement House, St. Stephen's Community House, and Godman Guild—also received grants for capital campaigns and capital improvements. Each neighborhood serves a minority and white, low-income population with many families existing at or below poverty level. Neighborhood leaders agree that the existence of new and improved facilities and quality programs for these neighborhoods helped create an environment favorable to neighborhood improvement. The South Side Settlement House has received much local and national attention because of its imaginative and noninstitutional architectural design. Barbara Stovall, executive director of South Side Settlement House, described the BMIF grant as the catalyst that helped ensure the building of the new facility. She also commended the BMIF board for not interfering with the plans for an innovative architectural design or with South Side Settlement's "taking a risk to reach for excellence." Neighborhood children refer to the center as "the castle," and Stovall noted there has been no vandalism since the center opened in November 1980.

One program grant was made in this area to the North Area Mental Health and Retardation Services, a coordinating organization for 16 mental health agencies. Three satellite agencies received portions of the grant, which helped stabilize them and allowed them to obtain funds from other sources. The funds provided for medical and clinical psychological services and strengthened agency third-party bases of funding.

Children and Teenagers

This social service category received the largest number of awards. Eighteen organizations received a total of 20 grants, which represented over 15 percent of the funds awarded to social services. Over 95 percent of the grants were for capital improvements. These grants ranged from $5,000 to $50,000, representing smaller grants than in other categories. The only large awards were made to the Heinzerling Memorial Foundation ($275,000), Boy Scouts of America, Central Ohio Council ($235,000), and Hannah Neil Center for Children ($150,000). Each grant helped to purchase or construct new facilities.

The Heinzerling Foundation conducts a residential program for profoundly and severely mentally retarded or brain-damaged children. This organization, founded as the "Peck O'Wee Ones" in 1959, was until the mid-1970s privately funded. It historically had very little community-wide recognition and support and served a special and relatively small portion of the population. The establishment of the organization was due primarily to the efforts of one family, Otto and Mildred Heinzerling and their son Dr. Robert Heinzerling, the current director of the foundation, and their friends. The foundation serves a 34-county area of central and southern Ohio and is the only private, nonprofit facility of its kind that receives state funds for basic operating expenses. According to Dr. Heinzerling, the foundation is able to offer quality care at less cost than state institutions. He hopes its example will lead to more facilities funded by a joint effort of state and private organizations.

The BMIF grant was contingent upon the receipt of state funds promised to the Heinzerling Foundation and upon the appointment of a full-time administrator. These conditions were met, and the facility opened in 1979. Robert Heinzerling described the BMIF grant as the "ignition, the fuse" that brought the organization broader recognition, credibility, and status in the community. It assisted the Heinzerling Foundation in expanding services from a 32- to a 100-bed facility. The building is impressive, but more impressive is the quality of care. To see profoundly and severely mentally retarded children encouraged to develop to their maximum potential is in contrast to the tragic way society has historically handled such human beings.[3] The physical plant, equipment, and programs are specifically designed to meet the special needs of each resident. The foundation also offers respite-care service for children who normally live at home, but whose parents desire short-term care for them.

BMIF awarded capital improvement grants to several organizations serving the needs of children. The Hannah Neil Center provides residential care for emotionally disturbed children. The grant helped to build a new facility that replaced a building that was over 100 years old and structurally unsound. St. Vincent Children's Center, another residential facility for treatment of emotionally disturbed children, received grants for building renovation and expansion. The Childhood League, which works with preschool-age children with learning disabilities, received $40,000 to expand and renovate its school building. Action for Children, a major advocacy agency for children and the prime sponsor of the Columbus Day Care Consortium, received a small grant to buy equipment for the establishment of a Learning Resource Center. The League Against Child Abuse also received a small grant to purchase equipment

Inside the Heinzerling Memorial Foundation,
a residential center for the
profoundly and severely mentally retarded.

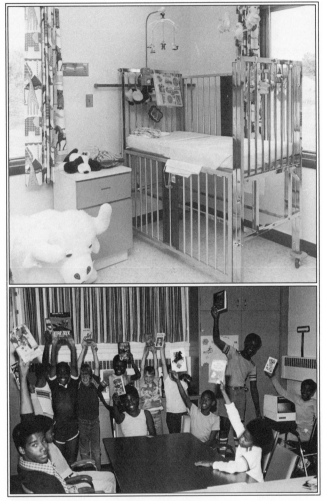

BMIF awarded the Salesian Boys Club a grant to help
strengthen reading and language skills of club members.

and other resource materials to help further public education, information, and awareness of child abuse.

BMIF grants also served the needs of adolescents and teenagers. Syntaxis and Starr Commonwealth for Boys are residential centers for troubled youth. Syntaxis works with girls and boys who are wards of Franklin County Children Services or other Ohio county welfare departments and are difficult to place in foster homes. The children live in community-based group homes that are cost-effective when compared to care in institutions. Syntaxis used the grant as a down payment for a fifth group home to serve youth who range from 12 to 15 years of age. The majority of the approximately 205 boys served by Starr Commonwealth are referred from juvenile courts. Besides other treatment and counseling services, the organization is an accredited school with a wide range of vocational training programs.

Huckleberry House is a 24-hour, seven-day crisis intervention center that provides shelter, food, and counseling for runaway youth. It received $40,000 from BMIF to help purchase and renovate a larger facility. According to reports from Columbus Police and Franklin County Sheriff's departments, there were approximately 4,000 runaways in 1976. Huckleberry House serves over 600 youths a years; 75 percent of them come on their own and are not referred. About 50 percent of the runaways are 14 to 16 years old and are away from home less than 24 hours. Almost 42 percent return home. The program was originally housed in a building with 1,300 square feet. The new facility has 5,000 square feet with space available for expansion. The significant impact of this capital improvement grant, according to Doug McCoard, executive director, was not expanding the program, but improving the quality of its services. The organization now has enough space to offer the privacy needed by the staff, youth, and visiting families for a program often conducted at a time of crisis and under a high-pressure atmosphere.

The Boy Scouts, Girl Scouts, and Camp Fire Girls received funds to renovate pool facilities at camps used by these organizations. The Boys Clubs, located in the near west side of Columbus, also received funds for a pool renovation project. This organization serves 1,300 youths in a low-income population area of the city. Since the pool opened in January 1981, 200 new members have joined the club.

The only two program grants in this area were awarded to the Salesian Boys Club and Family Counseling and Crittenton Services. The Salesian Boys Club is located in downtown Columbus and serves the social, physical, educational, and recreational needs of inner-city youth. The BMIF grant helped the club establish a Reading Improvement Center so that members could improve their reading and language skills. The center opened at a time when the Columbus Public Schools were curtailing special reading programs because of lack of funding. Officials of the club report member response to the program is favorable; approximately 28 club members enrolled in each ten-week session.

Family Counseling and Crittenton Services received start-up funds for group home care for single teenage mothers and their babies. The program offers child care and family life and home management counseling.

Almost all of the grants in this area were for capital improvements; however, the types of organizations funded were diverse and provided a wide variety of services for all age groups.

Handicapped and Developmentally Disabled

Nine BMIF grants went to six organizations serving persons with speech, hearing, vision, and other disabilities. All but one of the grants were used for capital improvements and equipment purchase. Grants to the Vision Center of Central Ohio were typical of the awards made to these agencies. The Vision Center received two grants totaling $82,160, one to renovate a branch facility and a second to purchase equipment for a new program. The equipment allowed the center to establish a Low Vision Clinic, assisting persons who are legally blind, but retain some sight.

The Central Ohio Radio Reading Service received grants to purchase home receivers for the blind and print handicapped. This agency offers 72 broadcast hours a week with reading services provided by community volunteers. Arthur Schultz, executive director, reports that the BMIF grant allowed the organization to expand its services and to increase public awareness of the agency's program.

Two organizations received BMIF endowment awards. In 1979, Pilot Dogs, which trains and provides guide dogs to blind persons, received $80,000. This funding provided the organization with enough income each year to train three guide dogs and their masters. At the time of the award, Pilot Dogs was having financial difficulty and faced an uncertain future. Still, in 1981, the agency served 130 people in 14 classes. The endowment ensures funding to continue this service to blind people.

The other endowment was an award of $162,500 to Creative Living, which had developed a specially designed residential facility near The Ohio State University for young, severely disabled paraplegic and quadriplegic individuals. The facility is used to help residents reach their full potential in both education and employment.

A seeing-eye dog and his master, both of whom graduated from Pilot Dogs.

Goodwill Industries of Central Ohio and the Ohio School for the Deaf Alumni Association received the largest grants in the aid-to-handicapped category. Goodwill received a series of three grants from 1976 to 1979 totaling $286,000. The Columbus Colony received $321,000 in 1977 to construct a skilled nursing care facility for the elderly deaf. Officials of both organizations describe the timing of the grants as critical to existence of the organizations.

In 1976, Goodwill Industries was experiencing severe financial difficulties. James Puleo, executive director since 1977, says the organization would today be out of business without the BMIF grants. In 1976, the first grant of $150,000 to staff the organization and improve its finances saved Goodwill. BMIF gave Goodwill $50,000 in 1977 in support of a capital campaign drive to complete a new three-story rehabilitation center near downtown Columbus. The third grant of $86,000 allowed this center to establish a new program service, the independent living residential training program for the severely handicapped. The center now is devoted entirely to providing counseling, skill training, and job placement services to the handicapped. It is the only Goodwill organization not engaged in used goods collection, refurbishing, and sales. Puleo reports the organization has achieved fiscal soundness and provides quality services to about 1,000 people a year and places over 300 individuals in employment or advanced training each year.

The Columbus Colony was one of the most unique projects funded by BMIF in the social services field. In the mid-1970s, the Ohio School for the Deaf Alumni Association, the parent organization, developed an ambitious and imaginative project to build a national prototype community for the care of the deaf, deaf-blind, and deaf multihandicapped. It was the first time this organization had sought active support from the hearing community. Phase One of the project included an apartment complex with 106 units and a 100-bed nursing home, shelter house, and picnic area. Residents include both deaf and hearing persons. The deaf are employed in every aspect of administration and operation of the facility. The administrative staff of Columbus Colony later assessed the BMIF grant as essential to the building of the nursing care facility. The timing and size of the grant provided the seed money necessary to receive matching funds from the U.S. Department of Housing and Urban Development. In interviews, Dr. James Flood and other staff members stressed the capabilities of Columbus Colony for research on the special needs of the elderly deaf. Information on this topic, such as need for interpreters, is shared with other local, state, and national organizations. Columbus Colony officials stress the importance of peer association and the sense of community not available to the deaf who are often isolated in other residential and health facilities for the hearing.

Residents making Christmas cards inside the
Columbus Colony, a home for the aged deaf
in Westerville, Ohio.

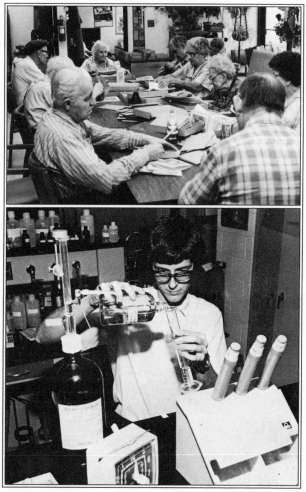

Research at the Children's Hospital Research Foundation.
BMIF awarded a $1.6 million endowment to the foundation,
the largest amount in social services and health.

Senior Citizens and Women

Approximately one-third of the 90,000 residents of Franklin County over the age of 60 live at the poverty level. Elderly people on fixed incomes are hurt severely by rising inflation and rapidly escalating energy costs. Elderly women are the fastest growing age group in the United States, and one-half of them have incomes under $3,000 a year.

The Senior Citizens Placement Bureau helps place Franklin County individuals over 60 years old in part-time employment to supplement their income. The bureau received two grants from BMIF to support and expand program services. The late Julian Marcus, the driving force behind the bureau, attributed much of the program's success to the BMIF grants that gave the organization status and visibility in the community and increased its ability to secure other funding.

The Women's Resource and Policy Development Center was formed in 1974 to address the needs of women in Franklin County. In 1976, BMIF awarded this group $25,000 to conduct a study of women's needs. The study found a major concern to be the displaced homemaker, a woman with few resources or skills who was required to earn a living because of divorce or death of a spouse. The study recommended the establishment of a women's resource center offering employment, financial, and legal assistance for women. In June 1981, BMIF granted $50,000 to the Metropolitan Women's Center to implement the legal and financial counseling service objectives identified in the needs assessment study. Grants from BMIF and The Columbus Foundation offered major assistance in establishing this innovative effort to serve women's needs.

Another grant to establish a new service for women went to Phoenix House, later renamed Choices, the only residential facility in Franklin County for victims of domestic violence. According to Sara Murphy, executive director of Choices, one out of four women suffer physical abuse by a spouse. Murphy believes that BMIF took a risk in funding Choices because it was a relatively new and not very popular cause in the community. BMIF provided $20,000 for start-up funds and an additional $30,000 in 1980 to purchase and renovate a new facility. The building provides a home for abused women and their children and privacy and confidentiality for staff and client. In June 1981, BMIF awarded $10,000 in program support to The Lighthouse, a similar shelter located in Lancaster for victims of domestic violence.

The largest grant to an organization serving women's needs was the $100,000 award to Planned Parenthood of Central Ohio in 1976. The capital improvement grant was used to upgrade and renovate facilities. The center offers comprehensive medical services for women on an outpatient basis. The Ohio Family Planning Training Center, a division of Planned Parenthood, is located in the new building and offers family planning training for personnel throughout the state. Planned Parenthood is a well-established organization with broad community support. The BMIF grant further increased the visibility of this agency in the Franklin County community.

BMIF awarded $260,000 to organizations that provide services specifically for senior citizens and women. This amount represented approximately four percent of the total grants awarded in the area of social services. Three of the grants to the Women's Resource and Policy Development Center, Choices, and The Lighthouse represented a departure from BMIF's principle of funding established institutions with broad community support.

Health and Medical Services

In the area of health, 19 organizations received BMIF grants totaling $2,746,318. This figure represents about 12 percent of the total amount distributed by BMIF. Sixty percent of this funding, or $1,608,576, was awarded in two grants (in three distributions) to the Children's Hospital Research Foundation. This was the largest amount given to any organization in the social services and health category and represented BMIF's entire distribution for scientific research. Most of the funding was used to establish an endowment, the income from which is being used for an expanded pediatric medical research program. The BMIF endowment grant to the research foundation was instrumental in securing a nationally prominent director.[4]

One interesting aspect of the endowment was that a large portion of it was originally in the form of 20-year notes for funds that Children's Hospital (as distinguished from the research foundation) had borrowed from BMI in 1973 to complete an expansion project. BMIF received the notes as part of the founding contribution, and the loan was paid off in 1980.

Most of the remaining health and medical services distribution was divided between capital improvement and program grants given to six organizations: American Red Cross, Central Ohio Heart Chapter, Harding Hospital, ECCO Family Health Center, Mid-Ohio Health Planning Federation, and Isabelle Ridgway Home for the Aged. A total of $96,000 was awarded for two studies.

The largest capital grant went to the Mid-Ohio Health Planning Federation, a comprehensive health planning organization for the 15-county area of central Ohio. The BMIF grant was used as a down payment for the construction of new headquarters, making the federation the only one in the country to own its own building. When the agency recently terminated, the building was taken over by the Central Ohio Lung Association.

The Isabelle Ridgway Home for the Aged received $300,000, the largest program grant in the health area. The home is a skilled nursing care facility serving a primarily indigent black population. The BMIF grant was used for start-up funds for the facility. Richard Blackenberry, then administrator of the Isabelle Ridgway Home, described the timing of the grant as critical and "a life raft."

The ECCO Family Health Center was a financially troubled organization serving a primarily black population on the near eastside of Columbus. The receipt of BMIF's grant of $50,000 was contingent upon the center receiving a Robert Woods Johnson management system grant. Jewell Barron, executive director of ECCO, credited both grants for the center's fiscal soundness and improved quality of programming. The BMIF grant provided for an expanded pediatrics department and full-time adult care facilities. ECCO was able to renovate and refurbish three floors instead of the one floor originally proposed in its application to BMIF.

The organization that received the most unusual and speculative grant from BMIF in the health care field failed to survive. The New Wineskins Center for Research and Development, renamed Health Care Plus, was planned as a national prototype health and educational training center using the holistic approach to medical care. BMIF's $42,000 grant was used for research and program development. The program began in June 1980 and closed in May 1981 when the agency failed.

Grant Hospital and the Columbus Department of Health each received a grant to conduct research studies. The Grant Hospital study was to determine the unmet ambulatory needs of central Ohio, particularly as they related to improving health care in rural areas. As a result of the study, ambulatory services were expanded and management support services were added to a small rural hospital through an affiliation agreement with Grant Hospital. The study conducted by the city's Department of Health was designed to measure, monitor, and evaluate neighborhood health centers. The study provides a model for a quality assurance program system designed to upgrade and strengthen neighborhood health centers. Most of these health area grants demonstrate BMIF's interest in exploring alternative means of health care and supporting outpatient services and neighborhood health centers.

Conclusion

BMIF grants in the social service and health agencies assisted diverse programs and a wide range of beneficiaries. Their overall impact was to: (1) enhance the status and credibility of social service health agencies; (2) provide tangible benefits of long-term value to the community; (3) strengthen existing organizations; (4) increase public awareness of social service and health needs; and (5) reinforce the trend toward coordination and integration of services. Barry Mastrine, former president of MHSC, believes that as a result of BMIF, Columbus will be in a better position than other communities to cope with recent cuts in federal funding of social service and health programs.

The majority of social service and health grants were for capital improvements, but BMIF funds allowed about 20 organizations to provide new program services. Almost all the organizations that received grants expanded their existing programs, offering services to more people. A few programs funded did not add to or expand programs, but improved the quality of services offered. BMIF's pattern of funding viable community organizations and new programs within existing agencies reinforced the trend of private and local government efforts to stabilize, coordinate, and integrate social service, health, and medical services.

NOTES AND SOURCES

Notes

1. Metropolitan Human Services Commission, *Final Report and Recommendations of the Citizens' Committee for Human Services,* Columbus, Ohio, 1977; also, United Way Annual Report.

2. Interview with Frank Lomax and Gwen Gilbert, Columbus Urban League, Columbus, Ohio, July 3, 1981.

3. Tour of Heinzerling Memorial Foundation facilities and interviews with Dr. Robert Heinzerling, John A. Taylor, and Raymond Tata, Columbus, Ohio, August 12, 1981.

4. Interview with Stuart Williams, Children's Hospital, Columbus, Ohio, July 23, 1981.

Sources

Studies and other publications on the Columbus social service and health systems and their funding sources.

BMIF Correspondence Files:
   Agencies Receiving Grants.
   Board of Trustees Minutes.

Questionnaires completed by agencies receiving BMIF grants.

Publications:
   Metropolitan Human Services Commission, *Final Report and Recommendations of the Citizens' Committee for Human Services,* Columbus, Ohio, 1977.
   Metropolitan Human Services Commission, *First Year Report of Metropolitan Human Services Commission, Columbus-Franklin County,* Columbus, Ohio, 1977.

Interviews:

Community-wide Grants

   Glenn Esh, executive director, Volunteer Action Center, Columbus, Ohio, June 3, 1981

   Pat Marsh, public relations specialist, Alvis House, Columbus, Ohio, June 17, 1981

   Doug Rogers, executive director, Legal Aid Society, Columbus, Ohio, June 17, 1981

   Madeline Speiss, associate executive director, United Way, Columbus, Ohio, June 25, 1981

   Frank Lomax, president, and Gwen Gilbert, vice president of the Center for Change and Leadership, Columbus Urban League, Columbus, Ohio, July 3, 1981

   Barton Schacter, executive director, Jewish Center, Columbus, Ohio, July 6, 1981

Neighborhood Impact Grants

   Barbara Stovall, executive director, South Side Settlement House, Columbus, Ohio, June 9, 1981

   John Maloney, executive director, St. Stephen's Community House, Columbus, Ohio, June 16, 1981

   Robert Cooper, metro executive director, YMCA, Columbus, Ohio, June 25, 1981

   Nancy Shilling, executive director, YWCA, Columbus, Ohio, July 21, 1981

Children and Teenagers

   Ben Ussery, scout executive, Boy Scouts of America, Central Ohio Council, Columbus, Ohio, June 2, 1981

Dr. Robert Heinzerling, executive director; John A. Taylor, administrator; and Raymond Tata, director of development; Heinzerling Memorial Foundation, Columbus, Ohio, June 3, 1981

William Kinnear, executive director, Boys Clubs of Columbus, Columbus, Ohio, June 5, 1981

Doug McCoard, executive director, Huckleberry House, Columbus, Ohio, June 23, 1981

Rev. Terence W. O'Donnell, executive director, Salesian Boys Club, Columbus, Ohio, June 24, 1981

Handicapped and Developmentally Disabled

Arthur Schultz, executive director, Central Ohio Radio Reading Service, Columbus, Ohio, June 9, 1981

James Puleo, executive director, Goodwill Industries-CORC, Columbus, Ohio, June 23, 1981

John Gray, executive director, Pilot Dogs, Columbus, Ohio, June 29, 1981

Dr. James Flood, director of public relations, and Dr. Jim Heilman, project director, Columbus Colony, Columbus, Ohio, June 30, 1981

Senior Citizens and Women

Julian Marcus, executive director, Senior Citizens Placement Bureau, Columbus, Ohio, June 2, 1981

Sara Murphy, executive director, Choices, Columbus, Ohio, June 9, 1981

Health and Medical Services

Jewell Barron, executive director, ECCO Family Health Center, Columbus, Ohio, June 23, 1981

Robert Keck, president, Health Care Plus, Columbus, Ohio, July 7, 1981

Grant Drennen, associate director, Mid-Ohio Health Planning Federation, Columbus, Ohio, July 8, 1981

Richard Blackenberry, administrator, Isabelle Ridgway Home for the Aged, Columbus, Ohio, December 2, 1981

Stuart W. Williams, executive director, Children's Hospital/Children's Hospital Research Foundation, Columbus, Ohio, July 20, 1981

Social Service: General Interviews

William Habig, executive director, Mid-Ohio Regional Planning Commission, Columbus, Ohio, June 1, 1981

Alfred Dietzel, president, Columbus Area Chamber of Commerce, Columbus, Ohio, June 9, 1981

Fran Ryan, clerk, Columbus City Council, Columbus, Ohio, June 12, 1981

Dorothy Reynolds, vice president for program development, Metropolitan Human Services Commission, Columbus, Ohio, June 23, 1981

"

BMIF's educational grants...opened up quality educational opportunities to a wider range of central Ohioans

"

CHAPTER VI

Education

BMIF's stated objectives in the area of education were "equalization of opportunity, achieving and maintaining high levels of quality, and maximizing resources."[1] But the field of education offered so many possibilities for action that it was necessary for the board to select projects that promised, in the words of one trustee, "to get a very specific focus for a reasonable amount of money and not just pour a few drops into the ocean of education."

Two proactive grants, the endowment of the Battelle Scholars Program and funding of the Gifted and Talented Science and Mathematics Resource Center for the Columbus Public Schools, were characteristic of the board's efforts to get maximum results from a reasonable investment of money. In addition to substantial grants to higher education and private schools and efforts to ease school desegregation in Columbus, BMIF tried to find ways to improve the academic quality of public education in Columbus. BMIF's interest in this subject stemmed from the conviction that the quality of schooling available to children in Columbus and central Ohio would have a decisive influence on their future and on the growth and prosperity of the area.

Battelle Scholars Program and Higher Education

Earlier chapters have discussed the origins of the Battelle Scholars Program and trustee concerns for its continuance after the dissolution of BMIF. Operation of the program during its first five years, 1976-81, can now be reviewed.

Enrollment and tuition costs were the major factors taken into consideration when BMIF divided the original $2 million grant for the Battelle Scholars Program among eight colleges and universities in central Ohio. The size of the awards was not based on any precise formula or scientific calculation. The Ohio State University (OSU), whose enrollment was many times that of all the other institutions, received an award of $656,000, or 35 percent of the total grant. The next highest award, $330,000, went to Capital University. Franklin University, whose enrollment was underestimated, received a small award of $33,000 that was eventually doubled. Awards to Ohio Wesleyan University and the Columbus College of Art and Design were reduced because those institutions had previously received support from BMIF. In 1981, when the trustees awarded supplements to six of the institutions representing one-third of the original endowment, Franklin and Ohio Wesleyan universities received more than one-third in order to bring their awards into line with actual enrollment. The total endowment of the eight institutions after the 1981 supplements is shown below:

Capital University	$440,000
Columbus College of Art and Design	87,000
Denison University	351,000
Franklin University	108,000
Ohio Dominican College	176,000
The Ohio State University	876,000
Ohio Wesleyan University	281,000
Otterbein College	264,000

When the Battelle Scholars Program was announced in December 1976, BMIF provided general policies regarding recruitment and selection of scholars, number of grants to be awarded, and duration and administration of the program. The policies, together with an exhibit,

"Scholarship Program," became the grant agreement entered into by BMIF and each participating institution.

BMIF left screening, selection, and day-to-day administration of the scholarship program to participating institutions. It stipulated only that standards of selection be objective and nondiscriminatory and that Battelle Scholars must be: (1) bona fide residents of central Ohio; (2) selected on the basis of unusual strength and promise in their chosen fields of study; and (3) in possession of "qualities other than intellectual ability evidencing a high potentiality for leadership" as determined by the participating college or university. BMIF provided $125,000 for supervision of the program, a figure subsequently increased to $200,000, plus all funds remaining at the time of BMIF's dissolution. The funds were used for periodic review of institutional programs for compliance with guidelines, centralized publicity about the program, and coverage of the cost of an annual recognition banquet for Battelle Scholars.

From 1977, when the first annual awards were presented, through June 1982, 97 central Ohio high school graduates became Battelle Scholars. Before their selection, the college or university screened each prospective recipient. The majority of the selection committees were in-house, composed of administrators, faculty members, and representatives of the school's student personnel department. Capital University included a central Ohio media executive on its selection committee. In 1980, OSU added an alumnus to its screening committee "to assure a nonuniversity approach to leadership."

Selection criteria varied from school to school. Every institution knew the key objective of the Battelle Scholars Program was to select students with "high leadership potential." With this in mind, selection committees made every effort to keep grades in perspective. Committees used personal interviews, written essays, and active participation in church, school, sports, and other extracurricular activities as barometers of leadership ability and potential. In reply to a BMIF questionnaire, both Otterbein and Capital specifically stated that leadership qualities were of more importance than high grades. Denison and Ohio Wesleyan noted that a recipient must have a combination of good grades and strong leadership qualities. Ohio Wesleyan pointed out that its selection committees did not necessarily select the "best" students, that is, the ones with the highest grades.

Franklin University, Otterbein College, and Ohio Dominican College said their scholarship winners came from the top 25 percent of their high school graduating classes. The greatest number of examples of academic excellence came from OSU, where more than half of the Battelle Scholars were enrolled in 1981. Because of its size and stature, Ohio State

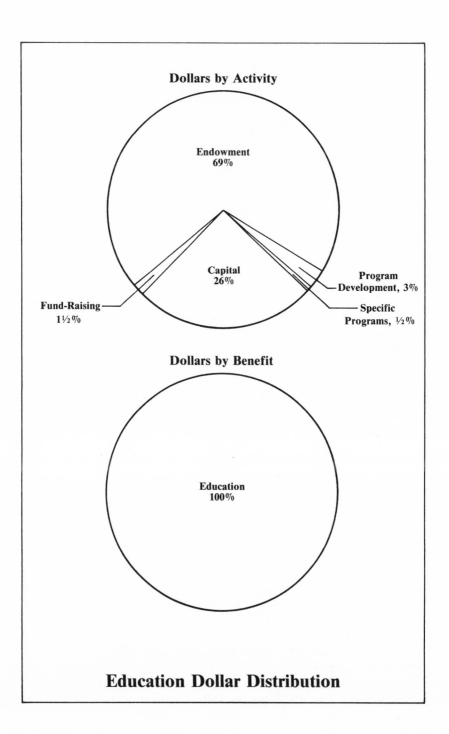

Dollars by Activity

Endowment
69%

Capital
26%

Fund-Raising
1½%

Program
Development, 3%

Specific
Programs, ½%

Dollars by Benefit

Education
100%

Education Dollar Distribution

could select its recipients from a relatively large pool of qualified applicants. In fact, during the first four years of the Battelle Scholars Program, all 43 of OSU's recipients were in the top five percent of their high school graduating classes. Twenty-seven of the 43 were valedictorians, six were salutatorians.

In an effort to respond to the objection that OSU's selection process put undue emphasis on scholarship, C. Grey Austin, university honors director, explained the methods Ohio State used to try to balance intellectual promise with potential for leadership:

> We begin with a pool of several hundred students recommended by high schools or identified from admissions and financial aid applications. Using academic indicators, we reduce the list to 100-150. Then from more complete dossiers, which include lists of activities and recommendations as well as high school transcripts, we select approximately 40 persons to be interviewed. In the interview we seek to identify such qualities of leadership as ability to express oneself spontaneously, ability to get along with others, poise, sensitivity to both people and issues, perspective and judgment. We also try, with some success, to maintain representation among the counties from which our candidates come, and to include minority candidates.[2]

In 1980, BMIF sent the Battelle Scholars a questionnaire asking them to list their academic achievements, extracurricular activities, and work experiences. The results were received during the senior year of the first group of scholarship recipients and provided BMIF with an insight into the personal progress of each student.

The group was divided evenly between men and women, but there were few minority students. Business and engineering predominated as major fields of study. Of the 71 students who responded to the questionnaire, 15 had chosen majors in business administration, accounting, or management; 18 were in engineering; six were in premedical studies; nine were majoring in science or mathematics; two were enrolled in a prelaw curriculum; and six were majoring in a social science. The other 15 were enrolled in various courses of study, including the humanities, education, journalism, nursing, and foreign languages.

Battelle Scholars, who had in part been chosen for their leadership, became involved in numerous extracurricular activities, ranging from little or no involvement to a great deal of involvement. Many were involved in organizational activities in their residence halls; a few were officers in student government; many more were members and officers in social and honorary fraternities. Others participated in volunteer service groups, helping with blood donor drives and senior citizen activities.

Of the 16 scholars who graduated in 1981, six intended to enter graduate school, five wanted to go to medical school, and one to law school. Three planned careers in commercial art, nursing, and accounting, respectively. One began working full-time in the stamp company he had founded while in college.

At the 1981 recognition banquet, BMIF President Harvey Stegemoeller called the Battelle Scholars "a gift to the future of our community" and predicted "we will in a few years begin to appreciate the bounty produced by that gift."[3] In the Battelle Scholars Program, BMIF provided an enduring educational gift that not only endowed area institutions with a rich and rewarding group of student leaders, but also promised to provide central Ohio with years of dynamic leadership in the professions, the arts, government, and industry.

S herwood L. Fawcett, president of Battelle Memorial Institute, in an address to BMIF trustees as the foundation was coming to an end, said of the Battelle Scholars Program:

> For me personally, I think the Battelle Scholars Program is, without doubt, one of the most creative and valuable actions any group of people has ever undertaken, for it is an investment in our youth and, in particular, in the development of future leadership for our citizenry. In a democracy and in a free society, the leadership must evolve from citizenry, it must depend upon a continuing source of good leadership. This you have endowed in a major way for the Columbus community. The structures and other physical monuments we have erected will someday undoubtedly crumble and disappear, but the investments you have made in our youth and in our future leadership will endure.[4]

The review of the first five years of the program supports Fawcett's optimism.

On the belief that communities in the state of Washington where Battelle facilities were located should share, in a small but important way, the funds distributed by BMIF, the trustees established a Battelle Scholars Program at the University of Washington, Richland. Recipients were to be graduates of area high schools who wanted to pursue four years of study in science or engineering at the college or university of their choice. (This policy was amended in 1981 to permit scholars to major in any field.) Scholarships were to range from $1,500 to $2,000 per year, and financial need was not to be a consideration. The program was originally endowed with a grant of $75,000, but was increased to $100,000 in 1981. In 1979, BMIF also awarded $75,000 to the Pacific Science Center at Seattle to endow a program that allowed two science teachers per year to spend a semester at the center, working closely with center staff and students. The aim of the program was to provide teachers with training in current science teaching methods and to improve their scientific background.

An incoming Battelle Scholar receives her award from Harvey Stegemoeller, president of Capital University, while Thomas J. Kerr IV, president of Otterbein College, looks on.

BMIF's commitment to the Battelle Scholars Program, which accounted for almost 13 percent of its total distribution, limited its ability and willingness to respond to requests from colleges and universities for other kinds of support. In March and June 1976, before the Battelle Scholars Program had been submitted to the board, BMIF made three higher education grants. The Columbus College of Art and Design received $373,000 to buy and renovate a former automobile showroom and garage into an instructional facility—now known as Battelle Hall. The facility is used for classes in drawing, painting, and sculpture. Ohio Wesleyan received $159,803 on a one-to-one matching basis for purchase

BMIF Grants in Education

AGENCY	AWARD
Battelle Scholars Program	$2,000,000
Battelle Scholars Program	675,000
Columbus Public Schools	600,000
Columbus Public Schools	525,000 (plus interest)
Columbus College of Art and Design	373,000
Battelle Scholars Program	200,000
The Ohio State University Development Fund	200,000
Ohio Wesleyan University	159,803
Metropolitan School of Columbus	150,000
A Better Chance	125,000
Columbus Academy	125,000
Columbus School for Girls	125,000
Options	125,000
Six Pence School	100,000
A Better Chance	85,000
The Ohio State University Research Foundation	78,000
Battelle Scholars Program	75,000
University of Washington	75,000
Ohio Board of Regents	50,000
Battelle Scholars Program	33,000
University of Washington	25,000
Community Learning Exchange	20,000
The Rooney Fund	20,000
Columbus Public Schools	14,246
Franklin County Teacher Center	10,000

of a digital computer system, and $50,000, only a fraction of the amount requested, was awarded to the Ohio Board of Regents to assist in developing conferences and consulting services intended to upgrade instruction at Ohio's public and private colleges and universities. After endowing the Battelle Scholars Program at participating institutions in central Ohio, BMIF denied nearly all other higher education requests, including some which the board and staff recognized as meritorious. Denial letters explained, "The Board is constrained by its prior and public commitments with respect to the funding of higher education" or, putting the matter bluntly, "BMIF has done all it wants to do in the field of higher education."[5]

Two exceptions were made for programs that were located at Ohio State, but served the central Ohio area as a whole. In 1979, BMIF awarded The Ohio State University Development Fund a $200,000 matching grant to be used over a two-year period ($100,000 in 1979-80, $100,000 in 1980-81). The funds went to the university's Telecommunications Center, the principal source of public radio and television in the area, and to Friends of WOSU, a related but legally distinct, nonprofit, fund-raising organization. The center and Friends of WOSU succeeded in raising funds to match the grants, allowing the community to receive public broadcast programming that would not otherwise be presented due to lack of funds. In one of its last recorded grant decisions, the board approved a gift of $78,000 to The Ohio State University Research Foundation to develop, test, and offer, together with public school systems in central Ohio, a remedial mathematics course for underprepared high school seniors who wished to attend college.

Primary and Secondary Public Education

BMIF's activity in the field of public primary and secondary education was central to its educational funding. Tackling a wide array of education issues—from school desegregation to school finance reform—the foundation found itself dealing with questions that were crucial to maintaining a sound system of public education in central Ohio.

At the forefront of BMIF's effort were two large grants to the Columbus Public Schools. The first, a $600,000 challenge grant made in 1976, was to be used for construction at the Ft. Hayes Career Center—$100,000 was earmarked for construction costs at the center's Performing Arts Theater and $500,000 for partial support to convert the old army arsenal located on the grounds into a fine arts center.

The center's unusual program offerings set Ft. Hayes apart from ordinary work-study schools. One major drawing card was its unique program options in the fine and performing arts. The center was able to provide first-rate facilities for a select group of the area's most able students. Even before BMIF's gift, the Columbus Public Schools and State Department of Education, Division of Vocational Education, had demonstrated confidence in the project by providing $1,405,000 toward completion of the performing arts complex. The late Jack Gibbs, executive director of the center, pointed out that the center helped to resolve school desegregation problems by fostering a cultural mix of students.

In 1981, in one of its final grants, BMIF set aside $525,000, plus accumulated interest, to endow faculty at the Gifted and Talented Science and Mathematics Resource Center to be established in the fall of 1982 at the Ft. Hayes Career Center. Under a plan begun by BMIF and developed together with school administrators and representatives of the Columbus business and educational communities, students with unusual promise in science and mathematics will spend part of the school day at Ft. Hayes and the rest of the day in their home schools. The program at Ft. Hayes will be supervised by an advisory committee made up of representatives of parents, the school board and administration, a teachers' organization, and members of the higher education and scientific communities of Columbus. In addition to offering educational opportunity, challenge, and possible career advantages to the students involved, the goals included broader objectives. The center hopes to provide a catalyst for academic excellence, establish a school-community partnership for educating the gifted and talented, and enrich the Columbus Public Schools, thereby making Columbus a more highly desirable residential community.[6]

BMIF also responded directly to the community's need to come to terms with the issue of school desegregation, an issue that was brought home by a 1977 trial and finding against the Columbus Public School System for segregatory practices (*Pennick* v. *Columbus Board of Education*). BMIF sponsored grants to two organizations, the Columbus Public School Board of Education and the Greater Columbus Educational Foundation (GCEF).

BMIF made five grants totaling $138,000 to GCEF, an organization that facilitated the peaceful implementation of the Columbus school desegregation plan. GCEF, which also received support from The Columbus Foundation and the Forward Columbus Fund, was the legal and financial vehicle of the Metropolitan Columbus Schools Committee (MCSC). This group was formed just before the 1977 federal court

Battelle Youth Science Program, Columbus Public Schools

desegregation decision and consisted of organizations and individuals that dealt with the public reaction and understanding of the anticipated order to desegregate the schools. MCSC was neither "pro" nor "anti" busing, but was a community support group interested in facing the realities of school desegregation rationally and objectively. Its campaign to educate the public was instrumental in helping Columbus adjust peacefully to the pressures of the desegregation activities, a success story that drew national attention and praise.

On a different plane, BMIF increased its support of public and private educational efforts by providing $20,000 in 1979 for program development at the Columbus Learning Exchange, a nonprofit workshop and resource center devoted to helping educators teach more effectively and creatively. It was the only organization of its kind in central Ohio and the only community-based learning exchange in the state. The center was equipped with a library of curriculum materials and the supplies necessary for creating innovative teaching aids. It offered a wide variety of workshops and seminars for teachers and parents. One of the exchange's objectives was to create an environment and a locale where teachers and parents could communicate about the learning process.

Other efforts to assist public education in central Ohio came in underwriting research projects at the Academy for Contemporary Problems and the Citizens' Council for Ohio Schools, an independent organization established to provide nonpartisan information about fundamental educational issues to public policymakers, educators, and citizens.

In 1979, the Academy for Contemporary Problems received a BMIF grant for $12,500 to provide funding for an empirical study of state and local school finance problems. This area of educational policy had become a top priority in Ohio and throughout the nation in the 1970s as educational costs skyrocketed, taxpayers revolted, and states and localities strained under the burden of increasing educational demands and decreasing real dollars. The academy study resulted in three published papers that outlined issues in Ohio school finance, tax diversion, and reform options in the distribution of state aid to schools.

In 1976 and 1977, grants to the Citizens' Council for Ohio Schools provided the organization with a stronger financial base and funds to publish one of its key publications, *Desegregation Update*. This newsletter reflected the council's desire to bring an objective and constructive "third party" force to bear upon the policies governing elementary and secondary education in Ohio. A 1980 grant to the Citizens' Council helped it to inform the public about choices available for reforming the school finance system in Ohio.

Primary and Secondary Private Education

Private primary and secondary education represented another area of foundation concern. The major thrust of BMIF's giving in this area was directed at increasing educational opportunities to low- and middle-income students and at providing a system of alternative education for area children.

Two foundation grants provided additional endowment funds at two of central Ohio's leading private preparatory schools, Columbus Academy and Columbus School for Girls.

Columbus Academy, a college preparatory school for boys, has provided quality education to area residents since 1911. The academy primarily serves the needs of middle- and upper-income families and offers programs in grades one through 12 to over 500 students. In recent years, the academy has become sensitive to the fact that lower- and middle-income families are finding it economically impossible to send their sons to the academy. The academy's 1979 financial aid budget amounted to only $50,000 a year, enough funds to provide 30 $500 to $3,000 scholarships.

This financial dilemma was mirrored at the Columbus School for Girls, a private preparatory school for girls founded in 1898. The school offers a full curriculum in grades one through 12 to almost 600 girls. The Columbus School for Girls had an even smaller endowment base than the academy. In both cases, the grant applications asked BMIF to support, through scholarship endowments, educational opportunities for middle- and lower-income students. The board gave each school $125,000 toward the endowment of their respective scholarship programs.

A continuation of the foundation's efforts to provide private educational opportunities to lower- and middle-income students was reflected in two grants to the Columbus chapter of A Better Chance, Inc. (ABC). A national scholarship organization incorporated in Boston in 1964, ABC is primarily concerned with recruiting and placing academically talented, highly motivated youth from low-income families in the nation's top college preparatory schools. Charter members of the organization included Andover, Choate, Groton, St. Paul, and Western Reserve Academy. BMIF trustees committed $85,000 to the fourth and fifth year fund-raising campaigns conducted by ABC's Columbus chapter. An additional $125,000 was awarded for scholarship endowment to support low- and middle-income minority candidates who attended Columbus Academy and Columbus School for Girls.

Two additional grants to private schools helped meet the unique needs of certain school children. In 1979, the foundation awarded $100,000 to the Six Pence School. The school was founded in 1965 by a group of Columbus residents who believed that the public schools were not providing adequate educational services to students with disabilities in the areas of perception, muscular control, language use, and social and emotional control. Six Pence has devoted itself to meeting these needs in creative and constructive ways. In the process of accomplishing this task, the school has been certified by the Ohio Department of Education and has grown from six students in grades one through six to a student body of 50. The school's early success necessitated a permanent facility. The foundation's gift resulted in the purchase and renovation of a building that could be tailored to meet the particular needs of this special school. This grant represented the foundation's only direct work in the field of special education.

A second gift to a nontraditional private institution of primary education came in the form of a $150,000 grant to the Metropolitan School of Columbus (MSC). This 1979 matching grant was used to provide partial support for a new school facility on Jefferson Avenue, a part of the Metropolitan Learning Community that had developed there. Central to MSC's educational philosophy was an effort to go beyond the constraints of the normal classroom setting and allow students to become involved creatively with each other, with teachers, and with a curriculum that stresses a continuing relationship with the city and with institutions such as the state capitol, Public Library of Columbus and Franklin County, Center of Science and Industry, and Columbus Museum of Art. New and innovative relationships were also fostered by the school's culturally, racially, and socially diverse population and in its emphasis on individualized curricula, personal involvement, and self-government. The school, however, failed to open in the fall of 1981.

Public Libraries and Community Support Groups

A final area of educational giving included public libraries and an assortment of educationally related community organizations.

There were two library grants. A $100,000 grant to the Public Library of Columbus and Franklin County, approved in 1976, provided funds to help purchase a computerized circulation system. At the time of installation, it was the largest on-line system in operation in any public library in the nation. This $215,000 system has produced significant savings by eliminating many operations previously performed by hand. The Westerville Public Library used a 1979 grant for $4,372 as part of a local match to federal funds provided by the Library Services and Construction Act (Title III). This money was to be funneled into the Columbus Area Library and Information Council of Ohio, a multicounty library cooperative serving central Ohio. Functions of the cooperative included expanding an interlibrary loan system, developing a standard resource card that could be used at all member libraries, and investigating a cooperative purchase program.

BMIF's largest grant to a community support group was $125,000 made in 1979 to Options: Adult Career/Educational Services, Inc. Options, founded in 1978, was an independent community agency that helped central Ohioans make informed decisions about educational and career choices. The agency trained learning consultants to give specific information about a wide range of educational opportunities, including vocational training programs, private trade and technical schools, avenues open to attaining a diploma, and traditional and alternative degree programs designed specifically for adults. In January 1983, however, Options went out of business due to the adverse economic climate.

The Columbus Area Leadership Laboratory and the Columbus Literacy Council were two other community groups that benefited from BMIF support. These grants represented efforts to help two distinct elements of the central Ohio community. The Columbus Area Leadership Laboratory received a $10,000 gift in 1976. This organization recruited and screened top individuals from all sectors of the community able to devote the time, energy, and resources to public service. Program participants paid for and attended a ten-month leadership training program. Meetings were designed to give participants the tools to be effective community leaders. A 1976 grant for $25,000 and a 1979 grant for $6,250 provided the Columbus Literacy Council with staff and program support to help some of Franklin County's 30,000 to 50,000 functional illiterates.

Conclusion

BMIF's educational grants had a significant impact on a number of broad-based community concerns and opened up quality educational opportunities to a wider range of central Ohioans. In the process, this support helped ensure that the region would not only have better public and private schools and educational services in the future, but also benefit through enriched educational institutions, more informed citizens, and a more effective and humane group of community leaders.

NOTES AND SOURCES

Notes

1. Battelle Memorial Institute Foundation, "Objectives," in *Criteria for Application* (1977).

2. C. Grey Austin to James I. Luck, August 18, 1980, BMIF Correspondence Files, Battelle Scholars Program—The Ohio State University.

3. BMIF Correspondence File, Battelle Scholars Program, 1981 Recognition Banquet.

4. Sherwood L. Fawcett, Remarks at the Battelle Memorial Institute Foundation Dinner, Columbus, Ohio, September 30, 1981.

5. BMIF Case Files 664 and 798.

6. A Prospectus for a Gifted and Talented Science and Mathematics Resource Center in the Columbus Public Schools, BMIF Case File 855.

Sources

BMIF Minutes.

BMIF Case Files.

BMIF Proactive Files:
Future of Battelle Scholars
Education
Gifted and Talented Program

BMIF Correspondence Files:
Battelle Scholars Program
Battelle Scholars Program—Capital University, Columbus College of Art and Design, Denison University, Franklin University, Ohio Dominican College, The Ohio State University, Ohio Wesleyan University, and Otterbein College

Battelle Scholars Program, 1981 Recognition Banquet

A Survey of Battelle Memorial Institute Foundation Grant Recipients. Impact: The Battelle Foundation, 1975-1981.

Battelle Scholars Questionnaires, 1980 and 1981

Interviews:

Albert J. Kuhn, former BMIF board member, Columbus, Ohio, May 29, 1980

Robert Gregory Mills, Battelle scholar, Capital University, Columbus, Ohio, June 1980

Julie A. Nehrer, Battelle scholar, Columbus College of Art and Design, Columbus, Ohio, June 1980

W. Ann Reynolds, BMIF board member, Columbus, Ohio, June 27, 1980

Van Durren Warren, Battelle scholar, Franklin University, Columbus, Ohio, July 1980

Teresa Lynn Wright, Battelle scholar, Ohio Dominican College, Columbus, Ohio, July 1980

Linda Susan Plimpton, Battelle scholar, The Ohio State University, Columbus, Ohio, July 1980

Kaye Louise Fritz, Battelle scholar, Ohio Wesleyan University, Columbus, Ohio, July 1980

Kris Andrew Lehman, Battelle scholar, Otterbein College, Columbus, Ohio, July 1980

Jack Gibbs, executive director, Ft. Hayes Career Center, Columbus, Ohio, November 14, 1980

Hon. Robert Duncan, judge, Federal District Court, Columbus, Ohio, December 1, 1980

Thomas H. Langevin, former BMIF board member, Columbus, Ohio, January 7, 1981

Edward W. Ungar, BMIF board member, Columbus, Ohio, October 1, 1981

C. Grey Austin, university honors director, The Ohio State University, Columbus, Ohio, October 9, 1981

Edward Q. Moulton, chancellor, Ohio Board of Regents, Columbus, Ohio, October 11, 1981 (telephone)

Howard Merriman, assistant superintendent, Columbus Public Schools, Columbus, Ohio, October 13, 1981 (telephone)

Terry Roark, associate provost, The Ohio State University, Columbus, Ohio, October 14, 1981

Harvey Stegemoeller, BMIF board member, Columbus, Ohio, October 19, 1981

Rowland Brown, president, OCLC, Columbus, Ohio, October 19, 1981 (telephone)

"BMIF's civic grants were characterized by an effort to increase the quality of urban life in Columbus "

CHAPTER VII

Civic Affairs

C oncern for "quality of life" helped to focus BMIF's approach to civic affairs, both in its proactive role and in its response to proposals for funds.

In the late 1970s, when the foundation was in operation, Columbus was experiencing new growth in metropolitan development, particularly in the downtown area. These development plans were the result of the strong private economic growth and public initiatives so evident in the community in the early 1970s. It should be remembered as well that federal policy encouraged the use of grant programs for urban development.

Downtown Development

T wo of BMIF's major grants had a specific impact on the development of downtown Columbus. A grant to fund construction of the

Centrum, located within the downtown Capitol South development, came early in the foundation's history. It was followed, much later, by a grant to construct the Battelle Riverfront Park. The Riverfront Park grant was one of the last grants made by the foundation, and represented one of the foundation's proactive gifts. Both of these projects emphasized appearance and recreation in the downtown area.

The Capitol South Project was encouraged by the city of Columbus and made possible by state and federal law. On the federal level, an "impacted" cities bill, passed in the early 1970s, authorized the formation of private, nonprofit redevelopment companies that could call upon local government powers of eminent domain. Ohio law also offered a good vehicle for urban redevelopment.

As legal channels to encourage urban development were opening, there was also evidence that private initiative in the community was growing. To further this movement, in 1972 Mayor Tom Moody created a task force of distinguished citizens to study the possibility of redeveloping three square blocks of downtown Columbus located directly south of the state capitol. These 15.7 acres had boundaries of State Street on the north, Main Street on the south, High Street on the west, and Third Street on the east. This was to become the Capitol South Project area.

On July 5, 1974, the Capitol South Community Urban Redevelopment Corporation was incorporated, and in 1977 the Capitol South Association was created to carry out the educational and charitable purposes of the corporation.

Capitol South planned a complex of retail, entertainment, and cultural activities, as well as restaurants, a hotel, and residential and commercial facilities. With its development plans in mind, Capitol South applied for an Economic Development Administration (EDA) grant to cover the major cost of constructing the two-acre urban park complex. It then applied to BMIF for $344,925 of matching funds to attract the federal money to be used to construct the Centrum, a sunken plaza located at the center of the proposed urban park complex.

The foundation made the grant with various contingencies on tax status, ownership, and the securing of the matching federal funds. By the end of 1977, Capitol South was able to secure $3,769,600 from EDA and funds from the U.S. Department of the Interior's Bureau of Outdoor Recreation. The Centrum has already proven to be a valuable recreational facility in downtown Columbus, but it has also been a visible symbol of Capitol South's potential.

There has been a great deal of both favorable and unfavorable publicity about Capitol South in recent years, reflecting the complication of attracting developers and obtaining government grant moneys. But the

Battelle Riverfront Park

city of Columbus has continued to support the Capitol South concept. By 1981, the city had committed nearly $30 million to the project, and the anticipated investment in Capitol South ranged from $200 million to about $400 million. The forecast several years earlier had been from $100 million to $200 million.[1] Mayor Moody saw the Centrum and BMIF's role in its construction as a "crucial element within the framework of the entire project plan."[2]

Potential recreational use and aesthetic appeal in the downtown area were merged with one of BMIF's last grants, a $500,000 award to the city of Columbus for development of the Riverfront Park. The proposal to BMIF by the city's Department of Recreation and Parks emphasized that the Riverfront Park was essential to revitalizing the waterfront. The construction of a park would also lead to replacement of unsightly concrete parking areas with green lawns and terraces, flower beds, water ponds, trees, and shrubs. The park would also encourage other activities along the waterfront.

As indicated earlier, the city's Riverfront Park attracted the attention of James I. Luck, BMIF's executive director in 1980-81. He saw the park as a "highly visible and significant step in downtown development." Mel Dodge, director of the Department of Recreation and Parks, echoed that sentiment in his appreciation of the initiative shown by BMIF in encouraging the city to apply for the BMIF funds.[3]

The BMIF grant for $500,000 was contingent upon the city first securing $1 million. The city's offer to name the park Battelle Riverfront Park was also written into the grant. Columbus City Council, on April 27, 1981, authorized the city to issue notes for $1 million to develop the park. There is no doubt that the BMIF matching grant was instrumental in securing the city's commitment.[4] By the fall of 1981, bids for construction of the park had been received, and ground was to be broken in December.

A small BMIF grant to the Development Committee for Greater Columbus was made in 1979 for partial support of a study of the feasibility of hosting a world exposition in Columbus in 1992. The event would come 500 years after Columbus discovered America. By the fall of 1981, a formal proposal for the exposition had been developed, although Chicago has since been selected.

BMIF also provided a $55,000 grant to the Junior League in 1976 to assist with the restoration of the Kelton House on East Town Street. Formerly owned by the late Grace Kelton and built in 1852, the house has significant historical value, due in part to its Greek revival architectural style. After restoring the home, the Junior League opened it to the public for tours and meetings. The restoration of Kelton House has been help-

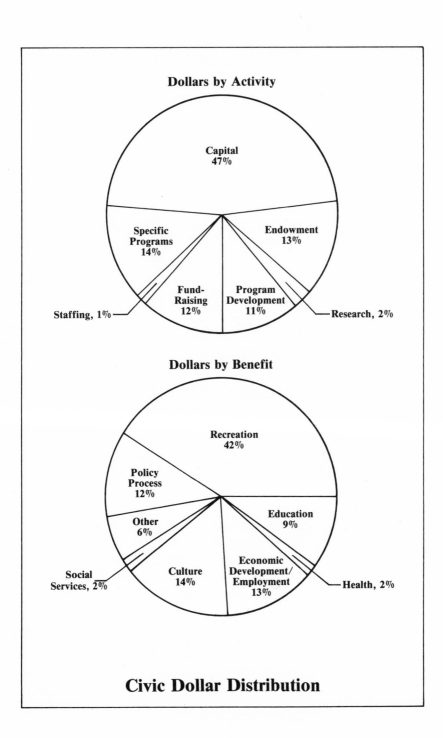

Dollars by Activity

- Capital 47%
- Endowment 13%
- Specific Programs 14%
- Fund-Raising 12%
- Program Development 11%
- Staffing, 1%
- Research, 2%

Dollars by Benefit

- Recreation 42%
- Policy Process 12%
- Other 6%
- Education 9%
- Social Services, 2%
- Culture 14%
- Economic Development/ Employment 13%
- Health, 2%

Civic Dollar Distribution

ful in the gradual redevelopment of other homes in the East Town Street Historic District.

Historic preservation, in general, was furthered in 1977 when BMIF granted $12,500 to the Mid-Ohio Regional Planning Commission to set up a temporary historic preservation office. The Columbus Landmarks Foundation subsequently assumed responsibility for that office.

BMIF Grants in Civic Affairs

AGENCY	AWARD
Metropolitan Park District of Columbus and Franklin County	$1,000,000
Center of Science and Industry	500,000
City of Columbus, Department of Recreation and Parks	500,000
Capitol South Association	344,925
City of Columbus, Department of Recreation and Parks	225,000
Academy for Contemporary Problems	210,000
City of Columbus, Department of Recreation and Parks	200,000
Center of Science and Industry	150,000
Columbus Neighborhood Housing Services	100,000
Public Library of Columbus and Franklin County	100,000
City of Columbus, Department of Health	75,000
Pacific Science Center Foundation	75,000
Mid-Ohio Regional Planning Commission	74,000
Junior League of Columbus	55,000
National Alliance of Business	52,265
City of Columbus	50,000
Greater Columbus Educational Foundation	50,000
Columbus Regional Information Service	49,048
Greater Columbus Educational Foundation	45,000
Ohio Historical Society	43,000
City of Columbus, Department of Recreation and Parks	35,000
Village of Urbancrest	35,000
Center of Science and Industry	34,182
Citizens Research	25,000
Citizens Research	25,000
Greater Columbus Educational Foundation	25,000
Ohio Academy of Science	25,000
Women's Resource and Policy Development Center	25,000
Ohio Citizens' Council for Health and Welfare	20,000
Madison Township Trustees	15,000
Ohio Citizens' Council for Health and Welfare	15,000

League of Women Voters Education Fund	13,325
Citizens' Council for Ohio Schools	12,920
Academy for Contemporary Problems	12,500
Mid-Ohio Regional Planning Commission	12,500
Development Committee for Greater Columbus	10,500
City of Columbus, Department of Development	10,000
Columbus Jaycees Youth Foundation	10,000
Columbus Area Leadership Laboratory	10,000
Community Information Referral Service	10,000
Greater Columbus Educational Foundation	10,000
Greater Columbus Educational Foundation	8,000
Citizens' Council for Ohio Schools	6,000
Citizens' Council for Ohio Schools	5,000
Ohio Expositions Commission	5,000
Westerville Public Library	4,372
American Chemical Society	1,200

Metropolitan Development

As mentioned earlier, the BMIF board was concerned with the city's development within the downtown area and the suburbs. Evidence of this was the largest civic grant made by BMIF. The Metropolitan Park District of Columbus and Franklin County received $1 million for the development of Darby Creek Park through the purchase of over 2,400 acres of land.

By the early 1970s, an expanding central Ohio population was pushing park services to the limit. This was further complicated by the absence of a full service park within 50 miles of Columbus. The Metropolitan Park District Board, responsible for the area parks outside the city of Columbus, turned to BMIF with a request to expand Darby Creek Metropolitan Park, a 369-acre park on the southwest side of Franklin County. The rationale for the request was based on the fact that the possibility of obtaining future county support was remote, despite the future southwest side's lack of adequate recreation facilities. Local support allowed Big Darby Creek to be designated a scenic river since it was the region's last free-flowing stream. Such designation would halt action on a proposed U.S. Corps of Engineers dam project on the creek and would open up 800 acres of government land for possible incorporation into the park system.

In 1976, with the support of the Columbus Area Chamber of Commerce, an organization that regarded park lands and facilities as essential to central Ohio's future growth and development, Edward Hutchins, director-secretary of the Metropolitan Park District, proposed that BMIF award the district a grant of $1.85 million over a four-year period to bring matching federal funds and other grants for the land purchases.

In granting the $1 million to be used as matching funds for the proposed Battelle-Darby Creek Metro Park, the BMIF board was praised by community leaders. In addition, the grant set off a determined and enthusiastic effort by the park board. The carefully constructed plans went forward following the grant award in late 1976. In spite of the complexity of acquiring many different parcels of private property for development of the park, progress has been fairly smooth.

The $1 million BMIF grant for the park was responsible for helping bring grants from the U.S. Department of the Interior's Bureau of Outdoor Recreation and the Land and Water Conservation Fund. These additional grants totaled $3.7 million. In addition, nearly $800,000 was raised by the Metropolitan Park Board from public and private sources. These funds, together with the BMIF grant, brought the total land investment to $5.43 million by late 1981, including some land yet to be secured. By that time, the total acreage of the park had been expanded to nearly 3,000 acres, close to the estimate made when the BMIF grant was obtained.

Due to these efforts, Darby Creek was extended to run 5.3 miles and represented the last free-flowing stream in Franklin County. In addition, the recreational potential at Battelle-Darby Creek Metro Park is impressive. Hutchins forecast that on a Sunday or holiday, the expanded park will be able to serve 20,000 to 25,000 people. In comparison, the Metropolitan Park's east-end Blacklick Park serves up to 10,000 people on a holiday or weekend day.[5]

Nature trails, a canoe livery, picnic areas, and other recreation areas, along with the conservation of natural beauty, add to the value and importance of the facility. Battelle-Darby Creek Metro Park has also helped increase the value of land in the area around the park. In all, the BMIF grant to the Metropolitan Park District helped create a recreational legacy for the people of central Ohio.

Metropolitan development was further emphasized in several other smaller BMIF grants. The largest of these was a $100,000 grant to benefit the Linden community through Columbus Neighborhood Housing Services, Inc. (CNHS). CNHS is a private, nonprofit corporation representing a partnership of concerned neighborhood residents, representatives from local banks and savings associations, and local government leaders.

Big Darby Creek, part of the Metropolitan Park District of Columbus and Franklin County's expansion program. BMIF awarded $1 million in 1976 to this project.

Joggers using one of the many trails at the renamed Battelle-Darby Creek Metro Park.

The preservation and revitalization of the Linden community are their concerns. This all-out effort to combat residential deterioration was coordinated by the CNHS Board of Trustees, together with a five-member staff experienced in home improvements, mortgage financing, community organization, and development and a group of community leaders.

CNHS asked the foundation to help finance a revolving loan fund. The fund would be used to finance high-risk borrowing for improvement to homes in the Linden community. The CNHS project included: a four-way partnership with the city government offering aid in municipal services and code supervision; financial institutions providing mortgage money; local residents acting as the backbone of the agency; and local philanthropy groups contributing funds for loans to participants unable to obtain credit.

Other grants that focused on metropolitan development went to two local communities. Urbancrest received $35,000 for the acquisition of land for recreational purposes, and Madison Township received $15,000 to help with the restoration of its historic town hall.

Popular Education

The Center of Science and Industry (COSI) in Columbus received three BMIF grants totaling nearly $700,000. COSI, established in 1963, is a part of the Franklin County Historical Society and is funded in part by memberships and admission receipts. The center has also enjoyed the support of public and private funding from the central Ohio community, including Battelle Memorial Institute (BMI). In fact, the institute was the center's first major benefactor, providing COSI with a planetarium and planetarium equipment. BMI gave COSI a total of $485,000 in matching funds from 1971 to 1974.

In 1977, COSI turned to BMIF with a request for $1 million to improve and increase the quality of research, development, and implementation of exhibits and programs offered to school students and the general public. The late Sandy Hallock, COSI's director, emphasized that an endowment was needed. The BMIF board responded with an unrestricted gift of $500,000.

Earlier, COSI had received a BMIF grant of nearly $35,000 to provide matching funds for construction of a physical science and technology theater and demonstration areas. COSI subsequently raised an additional $30,000 and established the Battelle Mall at the center. It is interesting to note that COSI's expenditure of the funds not only created the new mall, but also highlighted a new need to find continuing sponsorship for the exhibits contained in the area. That has been achieved, and today visitors will find in Battelle Mall an attractive and well-equipped educational area for the physical sciences.

The impact of the larger, unrestricted grant on COSI has been significant. Before the BMIF grant, COSI's endowment was $330,000. The 1977 grant brought the endowment to $830,000. In late 1981, the endowment stood at $1.3 million. COSI officials are gratified that in four years they have been able, in effect, to match the BMIF money. Recent policy action by COSI's board established a formula for the management of the endowment that will provide growth through retained earnings. It also called for three percent of the total assets to be allocated for the operation of COSI each year. In the 1981 fiscal year, that three percent amounted to $39,000 of unrestricted dollars toward COSI's operation.

Finally, COSI received a grant of $150,000 in 1981 that provides about three-fourths of the funds it needs to host the International Science and Engineering Fair in 1984. The fair brings together 500 of the top high school science students from the United States and nine foreign countries. The five-day fair, to be held at the Ohio Center in May 1984, will be hosted by COSI and operated with the help of a local committee. The fair will also bring some 2,000 outstanding students and their teachers and parents into the city from all over the state and region.[6]

Popular education in central Ohio was also affected in a major way when BMIF granted $200,000 to the city of Columbus for an education center at the Columbus Zoo. The grant came at a crucial time in the history of the zoo. In 1971, the city placed control of the zoo under the Columbus Department of Recreation and Parks. Since 1927, the zoo had been administered for the city by a private membership group, the Columbus Zoo Associates. Inattention, a lack of planning, and insufficient funds resulted in an inadequate zoo facility in a rapidly developing community.

Mel Dodge, director of the Department of Recreation and Parks, took on this addition to his department with enthusiasm and hard work. Dodge took a personal interest in surveying other zoos around the country. He became convinced that the zoo must become an educational facility, "a people place," as he put it, not just a place for animals.[7]

Dodge approached BMIF for funds for an educational facility. When BMIF responded with a grant of $200,000, it was contingent upon the city's ability to raise the additional $300,000 needed. The deadline for raising those funds was September 1, 1979. By August 28, the money was

One of the educational exhibits BMIF funded for COSI

Jack Hanna of the Columbus Zoo with friends

in place; $300,950 from 51 donors representing grants of $100,000 from the Borden Foundation to $25 contributions. Momentum ultimately produced more, and $600,000 was finally raised.

The educational facility has a classroom, a laboratory, a large multipurpose room, divided spaces for lectures, and administrative and docent offices. The facility was in keeping with the zoo's educational philosophy, an effort encouraged by its imaginative director, Jack Hanna. On a Sunday or a holiday, about 15,000 people use the zoo and its picnic areas. The BMIF grant was clearly a stimulant for support and visibility at a time when the zoo's direction was changing to meet the needs of a changing city.

City Administration

A grant was made to the city of Columbus to establish a physical fitness center for police and fire fighters, a board action that was described in the "Winding Up" section. The $225,000 grant was to be matched by $275,000 from the city to allow the purchase from Capital University of the land and buildings of the former site of the Columbus Academy for $500,000. The 12-acre plot includes football, baseball, and soccer fields. The buildings contain a gymnasium, swimming pool, and various classrooms and offices.

In June 1981, toward the end of BMIF's grant activity, a grant of $50,000 was made to the city to be applied toward the expenses incurred by Columbus in hosting the 25th World Congress of the International Union of Local Authorities. Mayor Moody was the chairman of that organization. He was to host the 1,000 local authorities (mostly mayors) from over 70 countries, who gathered for meetings at the Ohio Center.

Civic Betterment

A number of relatively small BMIF grants were directed toward general civic betterment. They dealt with public information, public policy analysis, and research. Examples of such grants were $25,000 to the Ohio Academy of Science to distribute 15,000 copies of the academy's publication, *Ohio's Natural Heritage,* to schools and public libraries in Ohio. Another example was a $10,000 award to the Columbus Chapter of the American Institute of Architects that helped meet the cost of publishing *Architecture: Columbus.*

Conclusion

BMIF's civic grants were characterized by an effort to increase the quality of urban life in Columbus. In that effort, consideration was given both to projects in the downtown area and other metropolitan areas. Many grants encouraged the coordinated effort among public and private funding sources. In addition, the grants helped the community make use of available federal categorical grant programs. It is fortunate that the BMIF granting period, 1975-81, coincided well with the initiatives for community development that had emerged in the early 1970s.

NOTES AND SOURCES

Notes

1. Conversation with Tara Barney, Department of Finance, city of Columbus, Columbus, Ohio, October 5, 1981.
2. Letter from Mayor Tom Moody to Joe Madonna, January 13, 1977.
3. Interview with Mel Dodge, Columbus, Ohio, September 29, 1981.
4. Interview with Harmon Beyer, Columbus, Ohio, September 30, 1981.
5. Interview with Ed Hutchins, Columbus, Ohio, September 30, 1981.
6. Interview with Roy Shafer, Columbus, Ohio, October 8, 1981.
7. Interview with Mel Dodge, Columbus, Ohio, October 14, 1981.

Sources

BMIF Board Minutes.

BMIF Correspondence Files.

BMIF Case Files, particularly nos. 329, 343, 452, 597, and 829.

A Survey of Battelle Memorial Institute Foundation Grant Recipients. Impact: The Battelle Foundation, 1975-1981.

Interviews:

Harmon Beyer, director of finance, city of Columbus, Columbus, Ohio, September 30, 1981

Mel Dodge, director, Department of Recreation and Parks, city of Columbus, Columbus, Ohio, September 30 and October 14, 1981

Ed Hutchins, director, Metropolitan Park District of Columbus and Franklin County, Columbus, Ohio, September 30, 1981

Tara Barney, Department of Finance, city of Columbus, Columbus, Ohio, October 5, 1981 (telephone)

Hilya Konze, Capitol South, Columbus, Ohio, October 5, 1981 (telephone)

Roy Shafer, director of development, Center of Science and Industry, Columbus, Ohio, October 8, 1981

Hon. Tom Moody, mayor, city of Columbus, Columbus, Ohio, November 24, 1981

Personal Visits to Facilities:

Battelle-Darby Creek Metro Park, October 1976

Center of Science and Industry, October 8, 1981

Columbus Zoo, October 14, 1981

Various visits to Kelton House, the Centrum, and the area of the proposed Battelle-Darby Creek Metro Park

"

The decision to create a foundation to distribute over $22 million was a wise one

"

CHAPTER VIII

In Conclusion

BMIF was created in 1975 as part of a legal settlement in which Battelle Memorial Institute was required to divest itself of $80 million. The foundation distributed over $22 million during the next seven years, primarily in the central Ohio area. When the foundation was formed, Columbus was growing, in contrast to most urban areas in the Northeast. Its growth and development were a result of many things, but the city's demographic, physical, and economic characteristics were essential to that growth. These characteristics represented elements of strength and, in turn, produced changes and growth in the community's cultural, educational, social, and civic sectors. In the 1960s and 1970s, Columbus was coming of age as an urban community.

By operating in a lively, growing environment, BMIF was bound to have a significant impact. The board consisted of community leaders who "knew the territory." Under the leadership of its first president, G. C. Heffner, the foundation was legally organized, and administrative procedures were developed. The board established priorities, grant criteria, and hired a professional staff for the foundation. Two executive directors, W. Bruce Evans and James I. Luck, guided the foundation during its life.

The foundation board was proactive as well as reactive to proposals submitted to it. Initiative was used in granting funds in education, yielding important programs such as the Battelle Scholars Program and the program for gifted and talented science and mathematics students in the Columbus Public Schools.

In order to discover the needs and desires in social services and the arts, BMIF supported detailed studies before awarding major grants in those areas. Both the Greater Columbus Arts Council and Metropolitan Human Services Commission were strengthened in the process of those discoveries, as well as through direct BMIF grants.

BMIF awarded a total of 176 grants: 24 in the arts and humanities totaling $3.6 million; 80 in social services and health for $8.3 million; 25 in education for $5.7 million; and 47 in various civic affairs for $4.3 million. Grants made through 1981 totaled $21,911,799. Additional funds, including interest to the Columbus Public Schools and the final distribution to the Battelle Scholars Program, brought the final total to $22,227,427.

For every grant awarded, more than four were rejected. A total of 925 requests were assigned grant numbers and received some attention from the staff and board. Many other requests were rejected because they did not meet BMIF's grant criteria. Whether the board's decisions were always sound is, of course, a matter of opinion. Its actions were not always satisfactory to everybody. A comparative study of the 176 grants funded and the nearly 750 rejected shows, in the overwhelming number of cases, the board and staff made wise decisions. The opinions of community leaders who were interviewed generally echoed those findings.

A survey of grant recipients yielded positive reactions as well, tempered by some criticisms of the board's application of the grant criteria. Some applicants who did not receive grants were questioned, with about the same results. While some concern was expressed about particular board decisions, on balance, most of the respondents praised BMIF for what it did for central Ohio.

Findings

The decision to create a foundation to distribute over $22 million was a wise one. A different form of corporate giving could have been used. Distribution could have been made by The Columbus Foundation, a community foundation with a proven track record. But the formation of a separate, private foundation offered the advantage of considerable freedom of action with wide community involvement. The private foundation mechanism also made possible the development and retention of professional staff members who could center on a specific activity for a limited span of time. Either a corporate mechanism or an existing foundation would have involved certain long-term relationships that could have affected the behavioral pattern of the giver. A new foundation, a new board, and a new staff suited the situation, which if not unique in American philanthropy, was certainly distinctive. At a time when corporate and other private philanthropy is being challenged to do more, the BMIF experience testifies to the value of the creation of a private foundation.

The composition of the board proved to have been a significant advantage. Board members knew the community and represented many interests. Together, their institutional contacts touched a great many organizations in Columbus. One could argue that the board was not representative of various segments of the public. Yet, one community leader involved in neighborhood causes suggested that the challenge put before BMIF required people who had connections and were knowledgable rather than representative of the various social, political, and economic segments of the city.

Since the life of the foundation was to be relatively short, the major challenges laid before the board were how to pace and focus the giving. The board consciously weighed the problems it could impose in the long run if its gifts replaced, rather than strengthened, charitable contributions in the city. The history of BMIF documents a successful pace of giving, and one that appears to have strengthened charity and philanthropy in the city. As the foundation's activity came to an end, statements of concern were occasionally reported in the press about what could take the place of the stream of funding to which the city had become accustomed. Those reports have died quickly, and later discussions and interviews conducted on that point revealed satisfaction that BMIF giving represented more than a "party that was over."

The board's policy of providing matching grants was obviously related to the question of how to pace giving and how many matching fund drives were to be conducted in the city at any one time. The matching grant policy of the foundation was crucial and, on balance, it was successful. Problems of proximate cause and incomplete agency reports make it difficult to document and analyze with precision the exact amount of money leveraged by BMIF grants. It would also be difficult to trace the indirect effects of matching grant inducements. A survey of grant recipients indicated that recipients of BMIF matching grants had more than doubled the BMIF funds—obviously a minimum, but attractive figure.

Of more significance was BMIF's conscious and successful attempt to use its resources to encourage the combining of corporate, public, and governmental dollars. James Furman, executive vice president of the new MacArthur Foundation, with assets of up to $1 billion, recently spoke to a group of college presidents concerned with the decrease of federal funds for higher education. He emphasized that in the 1980s, the chief role of the American foundation might well be to use its resources to influence the greatest cooperation possible between public and private sources, particularly the corporate and government sectors. BMIF performed that task. While it did so with no premonition of what would happen to government funding patterns, it developed a pattern of public and private cooperation in this community that may well last into the future.

BMIF stressed capital improvement. Thirty-six percent of all foundation grants and 46 percent of the dollars granted went for that purpose. Even in the social service sector, where one might have expected a greater amount in programming and less in brick and mortar, BMIF put 56 percent of its dollars into buildings or other capital improvements. There was criticism of that in some quarters. It appears, however, that in the current state of economic recession, a number of social service agencies in central Ohio will be better able to weather that storm because of the successful capital fund drives in recent years resulting from BMIF funding. An agency can cut back programs, readjust, and survive, but not if capital costs eat up its available cash.

The board's chosen balance between capital funding and human needs was evident throughout the life of the foundation. Primary emphasis was placed upon lasting gifts to strengthen existing and successful community agencies and organizations. A price was paid for that: less funding went into innovative or creative programming.

In this detailed study of BMIF, evidence of the important role played by the foundation's staff is seen through the records of grants and interviews of grant recipients. Many instances of staff work with agencies can be documented to show a role played by foundations not so often recognized by the public. Foundation executives and staff bring expertise and concern to bear on problems that may or may not result in funding, but may have an effect. There were instances where some agency executives felt they were not given adequate attention, but they were the exception. By and large, the BMIF staff demonstrated the helpful role a foundation can play if it wishes. Foundations are in business to give and to help make it possible for agencies to be eligible and prepared to receive. The BMIF staff exemplified active individuals who were concerned about their community—stimulating requests and trying to make unfundable projects fundable if possible.

Closely aligned to that involvement was the BMIF decision to be *proactive*. That term appears often in this history because the BMIF board and staff were determined to exert leadership. However, the effect of proactive giving over the long run has yet to be determined. For example, the Battelle Scholars Program, one of the programs representing proactive giving, emphasized leadership as a requirement for the scholarships. Carefully selected students in Columbus area colleges and universities were helped, and while too early to evaluate the program, its early years suggest great impact.

In developing the Battelle Scholars Program, the board asked the advice of the presidents of the colleges and universities of the area. Perhaps each experienced the same dilemma: appreciation for the scholarship program and at the same time disappointment in the resulting limitation placed upon their requests for funding of other projects.

Proactive giving has both favorable and unfavorable aspects. To a foundation's board and staff, it poses a significant challenge. Proactive giving also imposes a significant obligation to be in communication with a broad cross-section of community leaders as well as those at the grass-roots level. The tension between receptivity to requests from others on the one hand and the impulse to initiate on the other is difficult for any foundation to handle. BMIF appears to have struck a creative and appropriate balance.

The foundation's impact upon specific sectors of central Ohio represented a major portion of this history. In short, the impact upon agencies is difficult to evaluate, something most foundation executives are aware of. BMIF made no attempt to formally evaluate grant activity on a continuing basis. In fact, this study is meant to do that.

Evaluation is a complex process. One limitation in this study, for example, was that only 68 percent of the grant recipients who received the survey responded. In many cases, their records could not produce the detail needed. As a consequence, other sources of information, including a variety of documents and a great many interviews, were needed to produce this evaluation. Rarely could a foundation focus to this degree on the evaluative process.

No matter how sophisticated an evaluation process, qualitative judgment is involved. It is obvious that BMIF had an impact in central Ohio. This study has traced that impact through the arts, social services and health, education, and civic affairs. The grants to the arts came at a time when there were a great many changes taking place, and the funding strengthened professionalism and quality. In the social services and health, the grants came at a time of increased agency activity and helped fund capital investment. Education, leadership, and gifted student programs emphasized quality and opportunity at all levels. In civic affairs, quality of life was a primary concern, leading to the encouragement of economic development, popular education, and recreation.

Battelle Memorial Institute, as the donor of the funds with which BMIF operated, had expectations for the new foundation in 1975. As BMIF neared the close of its existence, Sherwood L. Fawcett, distinguished chairman of Battelle Memorial Institute, thanked those who had served on the foundation's Board of Trustees:

> Your actions and accomplishments are a matter of record written across the central Ohio area in terms of good works and aid to many and varied charitable organizations. Speaking for the Battelle Memorial Institute trustees, I must say that we believe you did a most magnificent job. You fulfilled your charge with great compassion for our community and with great wisdom. We are very proud of what you have done.

When BMIF was created, there were great expectations by the community. Guidance was provided in the foundation's deed of gift, such as the use of challenge grants, grants to stimulate charity, and grants for specific programs rather than operating expenses. These are the criteria against which BMIF should be held accountable. This evaluation of BMIF grants shows that the foundation's board lived up to its charge.

BMIF was fortunate to come on the scene at an opportune time. Columbus and central Ohio were becoming an increasingly important urban area, and BMIF had the opportunity to help accelerate the area's growth and development. Columbus is a strong community, and BMIF had a part in making it so.

Characteristics of Grants and Grant Proposals

T he following exhibit provides information on each of the 176 grants made by BMIF. Each grant is covered by the name of agency that received the grant, a brief description of the funded project or activity, the year in which the grant was made, the dollar amount of the grant awarded, and a coding of each grant by type of institution (I), type of activity (A), and area of community benefit (B).

The figures provided the base for analysis of grant characteristics that were carried in the text. However, there were analyses performed beyond that used in the text. For the interested person, the use of the codes can provide some additional analysis. For example, one can determine the dollars requested and awarded in one institutional category and compare that against another. Using that as an example, the funded amounts as a percentage of requests in social services can be compared to the percentage in the arts.

The following code guides the characterization:

I (by institution)

1. Education
2. Arts and Humanities
3. Health and Medical
4. Social Services

5. Government
6. Civic
7. Other

A (by activity)

1. Capital
2. Endowment
3. Program Development
4. Research

5. Fund-Raising
6. Staffing
7. Specific Programs
8. Other/Unknown

B (by benefit)

1. Education
2. Policy Process
3. Recreation
4. Culture

5. Health
6. Social Services
7. Economic Development/Employment
8. Other/Unknown

BMIF Grants

Agency	Description	Year	Request	Award	I	A	B
A Better Chance	Broader base of support	1976	100,000	85,000	1	5	1
A Better Chance	Scholarships for minority students	1979	500,000	125,000	1	2	1
Academy for Contemporary Problems	Use of building by nonprofit organizations	1976	185,689*	210,000	6	3	2
Academy for Contemporary Problems	Study school finances	1979	25,000	12,500	6	4	2
American Chemical Society	Distribute science book	1977	7,400	1,200	6	7	1
American Council for the Arts in Education	Distribute arts study	1977	75,000	25,000	2	7	1
American Red Cross	Buy and improve real estate	1981	500,000	100,000	3	1	5
Ballet Metropolitan	Establish professional ballet company	1978	400,000	200,000	2	3	4
Ballet Metropolitan	Generate more finances	1981	30,250	24,000	2	5	4

Agency	Description	Year	Request	Award	I	A	B
Battelle Scholars Program	Endowment and administration of program	1977	*	2,000,000[1]	1	2	1
Battelle Scholars Program	Scholarships for students	1978	*	33,000	1	2	1
Battelle Scholars Program	Administration of scholarship program	1979	*	75,000[1]	1	2	1
Battelle Scholars Program	Supplement to student scholarships	1981	*	675,000	1	2	1
Battelle Scholars Program	Administration of scholarship program	1982	*	200,000	1	2	1
Boy Scouts of America, Central Ohio Council	New scout center	1976	315,000	50,000	4	1	7
Boy Scouts of America, Central Ohio Council	New scout center	1978	372,986	150,000	4	1	7
Boy Scouts of America, Central Ohio Council	Renovate swimming pool	1980	35,000	35,000	4	1	3
Boys Clubs of Columbus	Renovate natatorium	1980	15,000	15,000	4	5	3
Camp Fire Girls	Replace swimming pool	1976	55,720	25,000	4	1	3
Capitol South Association	Construct plaza in park	1977	344,925	344,925	6	1	3
Center of Science and Industry	Support exhibit mall	1976	68,363	34,182	6	3	4
Center of Science and Industry	Provide endowment	1977	1,000,000	500,000	6	2	4
Center of Science and Industry	Support 1984 science fair	1981	225,000*	150,000	6	3	1
Central Ohio Radio Reading Service	Program support	1978	10,000	10,000	4	7	6
Central Ohio Radio Reading Service	Purchase 300 receivers	1980	16,507	11,000	4	1	1
Central Ohio Heart Chapter	Buy mannequins and equipment	1981	15,000	15,000	3	7	5
Children's Hospital Research Foundation	Endowment for research	1976	3,500,000	1,501,743	3	2	5
Children's Hospital Research Foundation	Fund pharmacology/ toxicology center	1980	333,333	106,833	3	7	5
Childhood League	Capital funds for preschool	1976	55,000	40,000	4	1	6
Choices for Victims of Domestic Violence	Facility for Phoenix House	1980	60,000	30,000	4	5	6
Citizens' Council for Ohio Schools	Support second-year operations	1976	5,000	6,000	6	3	2
Citizens' Council for Ohio Schools	Desegregation update	1977	12,920	12,920	6	7	2
Citizens' Council for Ohio Schools	Support school management study	1980	23,800	5,000	6	7	1
Citizens Research	Expand research program	1976	48,250	25,000	6	4	2
Citizens Research	County finances study	1977	70,000	25,000	6	4	2

BMIF Grants (continued)

Agency	Description	Year	Request	Award	I	A	B
City of Columbus, Department of Development	Sculpture for Mt. Vernon Plaza	1979	10,000	10,000	5	1	4
City of Columbus, Department of Health	Quality assurance program	1976	100,000	75,000	5	7	5
City of Columbus, Department of Recreation and Parks	Build Education Center at Columbus Zoo	1978	350,000	200,000	5	1	3
City of Columbus, Department of Recreation and Parks	Residency for four artists	1979	70,000	35,000	5	7	4
City of Columbus, Department of Recreation and Parks	Fund Battelle Riverfront Park	1980	1,000,000*	500,000	5	5	7
City of Columbus, Department of Recreation and Parks	Recreation/fitness facility for service personnel	1981	225,000	225,000	5	1	3
City of Columbus	IULA expense assistance	1981	50,000	50,000	5	7	8
Columbus Academy	Scholarships for disadvantaged students	1979	250,000	125,000	1	2	1
Columbus Area Council on Alcoholism	Youth support network	1981	50,000*	50,000	4	3	7
Columbus Area Leadership Laboratory	Transitional support	1976	80,000	10,000	6	3	2
Columbus Association for the Performing Arts	Improve Ohio Theatre	1976	750,000	500,000	2	1	4
Columbus Association for the Performing Arts	Expand stage area	1978	350,000	251,000	2	1	4
Columbus College of Art and Design	Acquire and refurbish building	1976	497,486	373,000	1	1	1
Columbus Jaycees Youth Foundation	Urban Walls Columbus Project	1978	20,000	10,000	6	7	4
Columbus Junior Theater of the Arts	Complete capital improvements	1976	15,000	10,000	2	1	4
Columbus Literacy Council	Program development and staff	1976	35,750	25,000	4	3	6
Columbus Literacy Council	Salary of executive director	1979	6,250	6,250	4	6	6
Columbus Museum of Art	Capital improvements and sculpture park	1977	741,758	741,758	2	1	4
Columbus Museum of Art	Major sculpture	1981	250,000	100,000	2	7	4
Columbus Neighborhood Housing Services	Revolving loan fund	1978	150,000	100,000	6	7	8
Columbus Public Schools	Ft. Hayes Career Center	1976	1,100,000	600,000	1	1	1
Columbus Public Schools	Visits to desegregated school districts	1977	14,246	14,246	1	7	1

Agency	Description	Year	Request	Award	I	A	B
Columbus Public Schools	Endow faculty and math/ science center	1981	560,000*	525,000²	1	2	1
Columbus Regional Information Service	Equip audiovisual conference center	1980	78,903	49,048	6	1	8
Columbus School for Girls	Scholarships for students	1979	250,000	125,000	1	2	1
Columbus Speech and Hearing Center	Start-up services in north Columbus	1976	17,348	12,000	3	3	5
Columbus Speech and Hearing Center	New roof	1979	7,950	7,000	3	1	5
Columbus Symphony Orchestra	Endowment fund	1978	2,000,000	1,000,000	2	2	4
Columbus Urban League	Center for Change and Leadership	1978	1,000,000	250,000	4	4	6
Community Coordinated Child Care	Librarian for learning center	1976	13,750	10,000	4	3	1
Community Information Referral Service	MINET system	1981	35,050	10,000	6	7	6
Community Learning Exchange	Program development	1979	38,400	20,000	1	3	1
Creative Living	Endowment fund	1977	300,000	162,500	4	2	6
Crippled Children's Center	Remodel building interior	1980	86,406	16,000	3	1	5
Dancentral	Professional dancer salaries	1978	111,705	45,000	2	8	4
Delaware Speech and Hearing Center	Purchase building	1980	56,000	56,000	3	1	5
Development Committee for Greater Columbus	Possible EXPO in 1992	1979	20,500	10,500	6	4	2
ECCO Family Health Center	Remodel and expand center	1976	200,000	50,000	3	1	5
Epilepsy Association of Ohio	Program development	1976	37,500	37,500	3	3	6
Family Counseling and Crittenton Services	Unwed mothers program	1976	40,000	20,000	4	7	6
Foundation of the Columbus Chapter of the American Institute of Architects	Publish book on Columbus architecture	1976	10,000	10,000	2	7	4
Franklin County Halfway House	Accreditation for Alvis House	1979	3,000	2,600	4	8	6
Franklin County Halfway House	Program for mentally retarded offenders	1981	45,769	20,000	4	7	6
Franklin County Teacher Center	Teacher awards program	1981	60,000	10,000	1	7	1
Godman Guild Association	Park development	1976	147,385	50,000	4	1	3
Goodwill Industries of Central Ohio	Capital campaign	1976	191,566	50,000	4	1	6

BMIF Grants (continued)

Agency	Description	Year	Request	Award	I	A	B
Goodwill Industries of Central Ohio	Assist financial operations	1977	350,000	150,000	4	8	6
Goodwill Industries of Central Ohio	Residential training	1979	230,000	86,000	4	7	6
Grant Hospital	One-year study of service	1976	21,000	21,000	3	4	5
Greater Columbus Arts Council	Artists-in-Schools program	1976	52,500	17,500	2	7	4
Greater Columbus Arts Council	Employ executive director and secretary	1977	233,000	65,000	2	6	4
Greater Columbus Arts Council	Artists-in-Schools program	1977	35,000	35,000	2	7	4
Greater Columbus Arts Council	Technical assistance program	1979	125,000	75,000	2	7	4
Greater Columbus Educational Foundation	Community desegregation awareness	1977	50,000	50,000	6	7	2
Greater Columbus Educational Foundation	Fund staff and office space	1977	25,000	25,000	6	3	2
Greater Columbus Educational Foundation	Community desegregation awareness	1978	750,000	45,000	6	7	2
Greater Columbus Educational Foundation	Program development	1979	12,000	10,000	6	3	2
Greater Columbus Educational Foundation	Community desegregation awareness	1979	25,000	8,000	6	7	2
Hannah Neil Center for Children	Capital campaign drive	1976	166,675	150,000	4	1	6
Harding Hospital	Campus renewal program	1980	100,000	75,000	3	1	5
Heinzerling Memorial Foundation	Facility for mentally retarded children	1977	350,000	275,000	4	1	6
Hospital Audiences	Cultural events for hospital patients	1976	10,000	10,000	2	3	4
Huckleberry House	Purchase facility	1976	40,000	40,000	4	1	6
Intermuseum Conservation Association	Development of new facility for lab	1976	30,000	10,000	2	1	4
Isabelle Ridgway Home for the Aged	100-bed nursing home	1976	300,000	300,000	3	1	6
Jewish Center of Columbus	Capital campaign	1977	2,000,000	500,000	4	1	6
Junior Achievement	Remodel two centers	1978	60,000	25,000	4	1	6
Junior League of Columbus	Restore Kelton House	1976	225,000	55,000	6	1	8
Kenyon College	Establish arts festival	1980	150,000	75,000	2	3	4
League Against Child Abuse	Purchase equipment for education and training	1978	5,000	5,000	4	3	6
League of Women Voters Education Fund	Practical politics course	1978	16,385	13,325	6	7	1

Agency	Description	Year	Request	Award	I	A	B
Legal Aid Society of Columbus	Establish paralegal services	1976	13,750	13,750	4	3	6
Legal Aid Society of Columbus	Senior citizens legal services	1976	10,000	10,000	4	3	6
Legal Aid Society of Columbus	Senior citizens program	1977	18,000	18,000	4	3	6
Liberty Community Center	Construct day-care center	1981	64,750	30,000	4	1	6
Licking-Knox Goodwill Industries	Sheltered workshop items	1980	33,779	27,427	4	1	6
The Lighthouse	Start-up expenses	1981	10,000	10,000	4	3	6
Madison Township Trustees	Restore town hall	1978	15,000	15,000	5	1	8
Mental Health Association of Ohio	Project PAVE	1980	30,405	30,405	3	7	6
Metropolitan Park District of Columbus and Franklin County	Acquire 2,440 acres	1977	1,850,000	1,000,000	6	1	3
Metropolitan School of Columbus	New school facility	1977	390,000	150,000	1	1	1
Metropolitan Women's Center	Staff space and supplies	1981	55,000	50,000	4	3	6
Mid-Ohio Health Planning Federation	New health planning center	1979	150,000	125,000	3	1	5
Mid-Ohio Regional Planning Commission	Regional historic preservation office	1977	12,500	12,500	6	3	4
Mid-Ohio Regional Planning Commission	Coordinate transportation services	1979	133,500	74,000	6	7	6
National Alliance of Business	Youth employment worker	1980	52,265	52,265	6	6	7
National Committee-Arts for the Handicapped	Special arts festival	1979	12,000	9,000	2	7	4
New Wineskins Center for Research and Development	Holistic health center	1978	48,929	42,000	3	1	5
North Area Mental Health and Retardation Services	Community outreach program	1976	183,182	98,337	3	3	6
Ohio Academy of Science	Publish book on Ohio's natural heritage	1978	75,000	25,000	6	7	1
Ohio Board of Regents	Program development	1976	320,845	50,000	1	3	1
Ohio Citizens' Council for Health and Welfare	State government information service	1976	20,000	20,000	6	7	2
Ohio Citizens' Council for Health and Welfare	State government information service	1977	34,300	15,000	6	7	2
Ohio Developmental Disabilities	Statewide developmental disabilities services	1976	150,000	37,500	3	3	6
Ohio Expositions Commission	Remodel Fine Arts Building	1978	4,994	5,000	5	1	4

BMIF Grants (continued)

Agency	Description	Year	Request	Award	I	A	B
Ohio Historical Society	Education programs	1976	405,000	43,000	6	7	1
Ohio Program in Humanities	Match for program funds	1976	100,000	22,500	2	3	1
Ohio School for the Deaf Alumni Association	Columbus Colony	1977	365,000	321,000	4	5	6
The Ohio State University Development Fund	Telecommunications center	1979	300,000	200,000	1	2	1
The Ohio State University Research Foundation	Develop remedial math course	1981	83,584*	78,000	1	3	1
Ohio Wesleyan University	Computer center	1976	319,605	159,803	1	1	1
Operation Feed	Franklin County Food Bank	1980	18,000	12,000	4	7	5
Options	Start-up costs	1979	168,000	125,000	1	1	1
Pacific Science Center Foundation	Science education program	1979	75,000*	75,000	6	2	1
Phoenix House	Establish shelter for battered women	1978	64,476	20,000	4	3	6
Pilot Dogs	Training fund	1979	80,000	80,000	4	2	6
Planned Parenthood of Central Ohio	Equip outpatient center	1976	100,000	100,000	4	1	6
Players Club Foundation	Expand facility	1978	533,000	285,000	2	1	4
Pro Musica Chamber Orchestra	Start-up for management salaries	1980	15,000	15,000	2	6	4
Public Library of Columbus and Franklin County	Automated control system	1976	281,000	100,000	6	1	1
The Rooney Fund	Scholarships for students	1980	50,000	20,000	1	2	1
St. Stephen's Community House	Construct family community center	1978	430,000	100,000	4	1	6
St. Vincent Children's Center	Renovate interior	1976	200,000	30,000	4	1	6
Salesian Boys Club of Columbus	Reading improvement center	1979	103,959	14,000	4	7	1
The Salvation Army	Program development	1978	124,000	30,000	4	3	6
Seal of Ohio Girl Scout Council	Swimming pool	1979	100,000	50,000	4	1	3
Senior Citizens Placement Bureau	Program development	1976	15,000	15,000	4	3	6
Senior Citizens Placement Bureau	Rental supplies and office furniture	1978	10,000	10,000	4	3	6
Six Pence School	Purchase and renovate school building	1979	150,000	100,000	1	1	1
South Side Settlement House	Capital campaign	1976	250,000	150,000	4	1	6

Agency	Description	Year	Request	Award	I	A	B
Southwest Community Mental Health Center	Purchase property	1980	75,000	75,000	3	1	5
Starr Commonwealth for Boys	Counseling and clinical center	1976	135,000	25,000	4	1	6
Starr Laneview Center	Recreation equipment	1976	6,000	6,000	4	1	3
Syntaxis	Purchase two new homes	1978	100,000	10,000	4	1	6
United Way of Franklin County	Study social services delivery system	1976	249,790	200,000	4	4	6
United Way of Franklin County	Purchase building	1978	1,000,000	1,000,000	4	1	6
United Way of Franklin County	Supplemental contribution	1980	100,000	100,000	4	8	6
United Way of Franklin County	Operating fund campaign	1981	25,000*	25,000	4	8	6
University of Washington	Scholarships for students	1979	75,000*	75,000	1	2	1
University of Washington	Scholarships for students	1981	*	25,000	1	2	1
Village of Urbancrest	Purchase two acres for park	1978	35,000	35,000	5	1	3
Vision Center of Central Ohio	Renovate sheltered workshop	1976	150,936	43,000	4	1	6
Vision Center of Central Ohio	Equipment and training	1980	39,160	39,160	4	1	1
Volunteer Action Center	Conduct volunteer survey	1979	15,250	15,250	4	4	6
Westerville Public Library	Local match to federal funds	1979	10,000	4,372	6	3	1
Women's Resource and Policy Development Center	Needs assessment	1976	37,250	25,000	6	4	2
YMCA of Columbus	Capital campaign	1976	2,159,000	48,000	4	1	6
YMCA of Licking County-Newark	Capital fund campaign	1977	350,000	100,000	4	1	6
YWCA of Columbus	Capital improvements	1981	896,204	200,000	4	1	6
Zivili Kolo Ensemble	Fund three staff positions	1978	12,000	9,000	2	6	4
Zivili Kolo Ensemble	Equip Croatian Hall	1981	6,000	6,000	2	1	4

Notes:

1. In 1977, $125,000 was allocated for the administration of the Battelle Scholars Program by the creation of the Battelle Scholars Program Endowment. In 1979, $75,000 was added to this endowment, bringing the total to $200,000. Another $200,000 was allocated in 1982. At the time of distribution to the Battelle Scholars Program Trust Fund, net income on this endowment, which amounted to $36,878, was also distributed.

2. This amount was supplemented by $78,750, the interest accumulated by the grant funds between award and distribution. The total grant award, with interest, was $603,750.

* proactive; no grant request or request invited by BMIF.

Survey of BMIF Grant Recipients

THE QUESTIONNAIRE AND ITS ANALYSIS

The questionnaire that follows was prepared and mailed to 116 BMIF grant recipients from 1976 through October 31, 1979. The questionnaire sought to elicit evaluations of grantee opinions of the foundation, the impact of the grant on the recipient organization, and the financial and economic implications of the grant. Of the 116 organizations surveyed, 83 or 72 percent responded with reactions to 91 grants (some organizations received more than one).

The survey took place from January through April 1980, but additional grants continued to be made through 1981. Consequently, not all BMIF grantees were included in the survey. The respondents did, however, reflect the percentage distribution of recipient organizations by type of organization. For example, 43 percent of all recipients and 44 percent of those who answered the questionnaire represented social service organizations.

The questionnaire was developed over a period of time. The first step was to develop a series of draft questions. They were held against, and in some instances influenced by, the review of questionnaires and final reports from approximately 20 other foundations across the country. The draft questionnaire was then reviewed by Appropriate Solutions, Inc., a Columbus-based professional survey research company, to determine whether the questions were appropriately worded, understandable, and in the best sequence. The questionnaires were mailed in February 1980. In order to ensure anonymity for the participants, a post office box was selected for the return of the questionnaires.

Differences in sample (n) sizes occur from question to question. Several factors contribute to these differences. First, changes in personnel often occurred between the time of the grant and the receipt of the survey. Newer staff members were reluctant to answer certain questions because of lack of knowledge in the area of the grant. Also, some questions were not relative to a particular organization or to the type of grant received.

The completed questionnaires were used in several ways. First, they provided a picture of impact on the community and an evaluation of the operations of the foundation. Use of open-ended questions directed to the grantees provided some interesting insights. Also, the questionnaires were used again and again by project associates in interviews with selected agencies to stimulate additional inquiries that might not have emerged in the course of a normal interview. Hence, various answers to many of the questions posed appear here and in various impact chapters of the BMIF history.

Evaluation of Foundation Staff and Board

The first portion of the questionnaire dealt with general information about the organization. The second set of questions asked the respondents to evaluate grantee experiences with BMIF in the funding process. The results are shown on the following page.

When asked to evaluate the publicity given to their receipt of a grant, 83 percent of the 88 respondents felt it was adequate. While press releases on the award of grants were issued after each board meeting, press coverage may not have been as extensive in the perceptions of the award winners.

171

How would you evaluate the process you went through to receive BMIF funds?

Factor	N	Negative	Percentage	Positive	Percentage
Clarity of requirements	82	3	4	79	96
Paperwork requirements	83	1	1	82	99
Assistance from staff	83	1	1	82	99
Timeliness of process	78	8	10	70	90
Overall evaluation	326	13	4	313	96

One area in which there was wide disagreement among the grantees was on BMIF grant criteria and priorities. When asked to state what they thought of the criteria and priorities followed by the board in dispensing funds, 68 percent of the 76 participants responded positively and 32 percent responded negatively.

The Impact on the Recipient Organization

The next series of questions was directed at determining the impact of the grant on the recipient agency. When asked "Did your grant accomplish exactly what you had in mind in the original proposal?", 79 percent of the 90 respondents answered in the affirmative. Those who felt that the grant did not accomplish what they had in mind tended to be those who did not receive the full amount for which they had asked. No particular type of organization responded more negatively than any other, since those who responded that the grant did not accomplish what they expected were proportionally distributed among all types. In addition, 34 percent of the respondents stated that they experienced unanticipated consequences as a result of BMIF funds. Examples ranged from unanticipated staff needs as programs grew faster than anticipated to program consequences that had not been taken into account.

Another important consideration for each organization was what it would have done had it not received BMIF funding. The results follow:

What would you have done next if you had *not* received the BMIF grant?*

	N	Percentage of Answers
Sought alternative funding	63	72
Gone ahead with project	10	11
Dropped the idea	5	6
Other (includes waiting for a period to seek funds again or taking a longer time to develop the program)	13	14

Apparently the majority of organizations would have sought alternate funds if not funded by BMIF. The respondents were asked to suggest where they would have sought funds. The results are given below:

Who, if anyone, would you have approached for funding if BMIF had not been in existence?**

	N	Percentage of Answers
Foundations	61	85
Business	22	31
Service charges	3	4
Government	23	32
Individuals	14	19

With respect to additional areas of agency impact, such as services provided and people served, the figures reported are not definitive, since only 83 agencies (91 grants) responded, and many stated that they did not have the information available to answer the questions accurately.

Of the responses received, 69 percent of the grant recipients indicated they were able to provide new services for their clients. The 26 agencies that had information available indicated they served a total of 161,980 new clients. When asked if they had been able to expand or improve normal services, eight percent of the 84 agencies responding indicated that the BMIF grant had allowed them to do so. Twenty-nine agencies with information available indicated that 514,482 clients were served, including 76,462 new clients.

---

* There were 87 responses. However, several checked more than one response so the total N and percentage reflect higher values.

** There were 72 responses. However, most listed more than one source so the total N and percentage reflect higher values.

Financial Impact on the Community

It is somewhat more difficult to assess the financial impact of BMIF grants on the community. Most grantees did not keep records that could provide answers to the questions posed. Those able to respond provided data that at least suggest the total impact on the community.

In the area of providing additional jobs, 46 percent of the 91 respondents indicated that they had hired people as a direct result of their receiving a grant. The results of the survey indicated both short- and long-range effects:

Additional staff hired as a result of the BMIF grant:

	Part-time	Full-time	Total
People hired	63	283	346
People retained after grant	3	243	246
Percentage retained	5%	86%	71%

It is interesting to note that 86 percent of those hired in a full-time position were retained after the grant funds ran out, while 71 percent of all those hired were kept on after the grant expired.

A vital question related to the amount of additional funding secured as a direct result of receiving a BMIF grant. Fifty-two percent of the 88 respondents reported they had indeed received such funds. In terms of the actual dollar value, 38 reported that they had received $11,279,990 in matching funds. Since BMIF had allocated $18,188,661 during the period covered by the survey, this indicates a return of 62 cents on each dollar invested in the community. Obviously, that is not the full picture since all agencies did not report, but it provides at least some indication of impact in terms of matching funds leveraged by a portion of the BMIF grants.

Many grants given by the foundation were in the area of capital improvements. To determine the impact on central Ohio, several questions were asked to determine the square footage involved and the total expenditure of funds related to construction or remodeling. Of the 30 respondents in the survey who indicated a capital project, a total of 472,786 square feet were built or remodeled. In addition, 2,002 acres of land were purchased. The total expenditure in this area, including BMIF funds, was reported to be $25,758,315. Ninety-five percent of these funds were spent in the five-county central Ohio area.